Conceptual Framework of Education

Sunil Kumar

UGC NET, M.Ed, MA
(Education, Philosophy, Sociology, Hindi)
Assistant Professor
Pujya Bhaurao Devras Mahavidyalaya, Kanpur Dehat
Chhatrapati Shahu Ji Maharaj University, Kanpur

KUMAR PUBLICATION

Kumar Publication, Kanpur

© Copyright

Book Title: Conceptual Framework of Education

Publisher:

Kumar Publication
(Self-Published)
Kanpur, Uttar Pradesh, India

ISBN: 978-93-344-2215-3

Edition:
First Edition – September 2025

Design and Layout:
Sunil Kumar

Published via:
Kindle Direct Publishing
www.kdp.amazon.com

For Permissions or Inquiries:
Email: rohansinghsunil52@gmail.com

Preface

Education has always been regarded as the most powerful instrument for shaping individuals and societies. It is not only a process of acquiring knowledge but also of developing values, attitudes, skills, and a vision for life. The present book, *Conceptual Framework of Education*, has been written with the aim of providing undergraduate students a clear, systematic, and comprehensive understanding of the foundational aspects of education in accordance with the spirit of the National Education Policy (NEP) 2020.

This book is especially designed for B.A. First Semester students, keeping in mind their academic level and learning requirements. The content has been organized into chapters covering the **concept, meaning, and nature of education; aims and functions of education; factors influencing education; and its role in social cohesion, national integration, and international understanding**. While preparing the material, I have attempted to combine theoretical insights with practical perspectives so that students not only learn definitions and concepts but also understand their relevance in real life.

Special care has been taken to make the subject matter student-friendly. The text is enriched with definitions of eminent educationists, illustrative examples, and comparative tables to simplify complex ideas. This method will enable learners to grasp the subject more easily, encourage critical thinking, and strengthen their conceptual foundation. The book does not merely aim at helping students prepare for examinations but also aspires to inspire them to reflect upon the role of education in personality development, social harmony, and national progress.

I believe that education, when understood in its true sense, helps us appreciate our cultural heritage, embrace diversity, and prepare ourselves for global citizenship. The purpose of this book is to serve as a guide for students in their academic journey and to motivate them to value education as a lifelong process of growth, transformation, and service to society.

I am grateful to my teachers, colleagues, and students whose encouragement, guidance, and feedback played a vital role in shaping this work. I sincerely hope that this book will prove useful not only for undergraduate learners but also for anyone interested in gaining an insightful understanding of the basic concepts of education.

— Sunil Kumar

INDEX

- Concept, Aims and Importance
- Models of Pre-Primary Education: Dalton, Montessori, Kindergarten
- Present Status of Pre-Primary Education in India
- National Education Policy (NEP 2020) and Pre-Primary Education

Chapter 6: Primary and Secondary Education

- Concept, Aims and Importance of Secondary Education
- Present Status of Primary Education in India

Chapter 7: Higher Education

- Concept, Aims and Importance
- Types of Universities: Central, State, Private and Open Universities
- Present Status of Higher Education in India

Chapter 8: Guiding and Regulatory Bodies of Education in India

- Ministry of Education (MHRD), UNESCO
- NCERT, SCERT, DIET
- NIOS, NUEPA
- NCTE, UGC
- NAAC, IQAC, AICTE
- International Boards, National Boards, CBSE, State Board

Chapter 1

Education – Concept and Aims

1.1 Ancient Indian Knowledge Tradition: The Way of Life, Guru and Education

Introduction

India is one of the oldest civilizations in the world, with a unique **knowledge tradition** that dates back thousands of years. Education in ancient India was not limited to literacy or vocational training—it was a **way of life**. The aim was the all-round development of an individual: physical, mental, social, moral, and spiritual.

The system was based on the **Guru–Shishya parampara (teacher–disciple tradition)**, where the **Guru** (teacher) was considered not just a source of knowledge but also a moral guide and role model. Students (Shishyas) lived in **Gurukuls**, learning discipline, values, and skills necessary for life.

1. Meaning of Ancient Indian Knowledge Tradition

- Knowledge tradition refers to the **continuous transmission of knowledge, values, and practices** from one generation to another.
- In India, education was linked to **dharma (duty), artha (livelihood), kama (desires), and moksha (liberation)**.

- It emphasized **spiritual enlightenment, moral development, and self-realization** along with intellectual training.

Definition by Dr. R.N. Sharma:

"Education in ancient India was a process of leading the child from darkness to light, from ignorance to knowledge, and from mortality to immortality."

2. Education as a Way of Life

In ancient India, education was inseparable from daily life.

Features of Gurukul Education System:

1. **Residential nature** – Students lived with their Guru in Gurukuls.
2. **Simple living, high thinking** – Emphasis on discipline and modesty.
3. **Self-dependence** – Students did daily chores (cooking, cleaning, collecting wood).
4. **Holistic learning** – Intellectual, physical, moral, and spiritual growth.
5. **Integration with society** – Education prepared students to serve family, society, and nation.

□ Thus, education was not a separate activity, but a complete lifestyle.

3. Role of the Guru in Education

The **Guru** was central to the system.

- He was a **philosopher, guide, and role model**.
- The relationship between Guru and Shishya was based on **faith, respect, and dedication**.
- Guru was responsible for both **intellectual teaching** and **moral character formation**.

Swami Vivekananda's view:

"The true teacher is he who can inspire, enlighten, and awaken the power of the soul in his pupil."

4. Aims of Education in Ancient India

The education system focused on **all-round development**:

1. **Self-realization** – Discovering one's true self.
2. **Character formation** – Developing honesty, discipline, and truthfulness.
3. **Civic responsibility** – Preparing responsible citizens.
4. **Livelihood** – Training in agriculture, warfare, trade, and crafts.
5. **Spiritual upliftment** – Attaining moksha (liberation).

M. Hiriyanna:

"The object of education in India has always been not to accumulate information, but to develop the powers of human mind and spirit."

5. Methods of Teaching

- **Oral tradition (श्रुति–स्मृति)** – Knowledge was transmitted orally.
- **Memorization** – Repetition of hymns and verses.
- **Dialogue (संवाद पद्धति)** – Discussion between Guru and Shishya.
- **Practical training** – Agriculture, craft, martial arts, yoga.
- **Debates (शास्त्रार्थ)** – Development of reasoning and logic.

6. Subjects of Study

The curriculum was broad and balanced:

- **Sacred texts** – Vedas, Upanishads, Puranas, Epics.
- **Philosophy** – Nyaya, Samkhya, Yoga, Vedanta, Buddhism, Jainism.
- **Sciences** – Mathematics, Astronomy, Ayurveda (Medicine), Grammar.
- **Arts** – Music, Dance, Drama, Painting.
- **Physical training** – Archery, wrestling, horse-riding, yoga.

7. Comparison: Ancient Indian Education and Modern Education

Aspect	Ancient Indian Education	Modern Education
Nature	Spiritual, moral, holistic	Scientific, technical, job-oriented
Place of Learning	Gurukuls, Ashrams, Universities	Schools, Colleges, Universities
Medium	Sanskrit, Prakrit	Regional languages, English
Method	Oral, memorization, dialogue	Written, digital, interactive
Aim	Self-realization, character-building	Employment, social mobility
Teacher's Role	Guru as guide and role model	Teacher as instructor/facilitator
Relationship	Personal, emotional, spiritual	Formal and professional

8. Relevance in Present Times

Even today, the ancient tradition holds importance:

- Need for **value-based education** in modern times.
- Emphasis on **discipline and moral values**.
- Importance of **holistic development**.
- Role of **teacher as guide and mentor**.

- Preservation of **cultural heritage**.

NEP 2020 also stresses on **holistic, value-oriented and skill-based learning**, which reflects the essence of this tradition.

Conclusion

The **Ancient Indian Knowledge Tradition** treated education as a complete way of life. The **Guru–Shishya parampara** was the foundation of moral and intellectual development. The aim was not only to prepare individuals for livelihood but also for **self-realization and service to society**.

In today's world of globalization and technology, reviving these values can make education more **meaningful, humanistic, and life-oriented**.

1.2 – Concept of Education: Meaning and Nature

Introduction

Education is a universal process found in all human societies. It is the key to personal growth and social development. In simple words, **education means the process of learning to live a better life**. But education is not limited to schools and colleges—it starts from birth and continues throughout life.

The word **Education** has been interpreted in different ways by different scholars, and its **meaning and nature** have evolved with time and culture.

1. Etymology of Education

The term **Education** comes from three Latin words:

1. **Educare** – to bring up, to nourish.
2. **Educere** – to draw out, to bring forth from within.
3. **Educatum** – the act of teaching and training.

□ Thus, education means **to develop the inner powers of the child and guide him towards a better life**.

2. Definitions of Education

Western Thinkers

1. **Plato** – "Education is the process of development of mind and body."
2. **Aristotle** – "Education is the creation of a sound mind in a sound body."
3. **John Dewey** – "Education is the process of living and not a preparation for future living."
4. **Pestalozzi** – "Education is the natural, harmonious and progressive development of man's innate powers."

Indian Thinkers

1. **Swami Vivekananda** – "Education is the manifestation of the perfection already in man."

2. **Mahatma Gandhi** – "By education, I mean an all-round drawing out of the best in child and man—body, mind and spirit."
3. **Rabindranath Tagore** – "The highest education is that which does not merely give us information but makes our life in harmony with all existence."

3. Meaning of Education

From the above definitions, the **meaning of education** can be understood as:

- A continuous and lifelong process.
- All-round development of body, mind, and spirit.
- Process of socialization and adjustment.
- Training for character, citizenship, and livelihood.
- Development of hidden talents and potentialities.

□ **Education = Development of individual + Betterment of society.**

4. Nature of Education

The nature of education describes its essential features:

1. **Lifelong process** – Education starts with birth and continues till death.
2. **Dynamic process** – It changes according to social needs and cultural values.

3. **Bipolar process** – It involves **teacher (influence)** and **student (growth)**.
4. **Tripolar process** – Involves **teacher, student, and society**.
5. **Holistic in nature** – It develops physical, mental, moral, and spiritual aspects.
6. **Social process** – Education transmits culture and social values.
7. **Continuous process** – It is not limited to classroom; experiences of life also educate us.
8. **Value-oriented** – Education shapes moral and ethical character.

5. Table: Formal Meaning vs. Wider Meaning of Education

Aspect	Formal/Narrow Meaning	Wider Meaning
Place of Learning	Schools, Colleges, Universities	Whole life, every experience
Nature	Structured, syllabus-based	Lifelong, continuous
Focus	Literacy, knowledge, training	All-round personality development
Agents	Teachers, Institutions	Family, peers, society, media, nature
Example	Reading, writing, exams	Learning values, culture, discipline through life

6. Education as a Bipolar and Tripolar Process

- **Bipolar Process (J.S. Ross):** Education is an interaction between **teacher and student**. The teacher influences, the student grows.
- **Tripolar Process (John Dewey):** Education is a process involving **teacher, student, and society**. Society sets the aims, teacher facilitates, and student learns.

7. Functions of Education (Based on its Nature)

1. **Personal Development** – developing personality, skills, and values.
2. **Social Development** – transmitting culture, social norms, and preparing responsible citizens.
3. **Economic Development** – skill development, employment, and productivity.
4. **Cultural Development** – preserving traditions, heritage, and language.
5. **Moral and Spiritual Development** – cultivation of values, ethics, and higher thinking.

8. Distinction between Education, Training, and Teaching

Basis	Education	Training	Teaching
Meaning	All-round development	Development of specific skills	Process of imparting knowledge
Scope	Broad and lifelong	Narrow, job-oriented	Limited to classroom

Aim	Personality development, social adjustment	Efficiency, productivity	Knowledge transmission
Example	Moral education, citizenship education	Army training, skill training	School teaching

1.3 Vidya and Gyan – Difference between Teaching, Training and Education

1. Introduction

In the field of education, the terms **Vidya, Gyan, Teaching, Training and Education** are often used interchangeably, but they carry different meanings and implications. For a deep understanding of the **conceptual framework of education**, it is important for students to differentiate between these terms.

- **Vidya** refers to higher knowledge, wisdom, and value-oriented learning.
- **Gyan** refers to awareness, information, and intellectual understanding.
- **Teaching** means the act of imparting knowledge.
- **Training** focuses on developing skills and competencies.
- **Education** is a holistic process aimed at the all-round development of the individual.

This chapter will explore these concepts with definitions, examples, and comparative tables.

2. Vidya and Gyan

(a) Vidya

The Sanskrit word *Vidya* comes from the root *vid* which means "to know" or "to realize." It is not limited to bookish knowledge, but refers to **self-realization, wisdom, and the pursuit of higher truth**.

Definitions:

1. **Dr. S. Radhakrishnan:** "Vidya is that which leads man towards Truth, Goodness, and Beauty."
2. **Yajnavalkya (Ancient Sage):** *"Sa Vidya Ya Vimuktaye"* – True Vidya is that which liberates.

Thus, Vidya has a spiritual and moral orientation.

(b) Gyan

Gyan simply means knowledge, awareness, or information about facts, principles, or experiences. It can be theoretical (book knowledge) or practical (experience-based).

Definitions:

1. **Swami Vivekananda:** "Knowledge is inherent in man. Education is the manifestation of the perfection already in man."
2. **Plato:** "Knowledge is justified true belief."

Hence, Gyan is primarily intellectual and cognitive in nature.

3. Difference between Vidya and Gyan

Basis	Vidya (Wisdom)	Gyan (Knowledge)
Objective	Self-realization, liberation, value orientation	Awareness, information, intellectual growth
Nature	Abstract, spiritual, eternal	Practical, factual, and limited
Source	Guru, philosophy, self-reflection	Study, observation, experience
Scope	Infinite, life-long guidance	Context-specific and subject-specific
Benefit	Provides meaning to life, moral upliftment	Helps in solving problems, achieving success

□ **Conclusion:** Gyan can be a step towards Vidya, but Vidya is the higher and ultimate form of learning.

4. Teaching, Training, and Education

(a) Teaching

Teaching refers to the **planned and systematic presentation of knowledge** by a teacher to students. It involves explanation, demonstration, guidance, and evaluation.

Definitions:

- **Curtis:** "Teaching is an activity which enables the learner to learn."
- **Gates:** "Teaching is stimulation, guidance, direction, and encouragement of learning."

Example: A history teacher explaining the causes of the Revolt of 1857.

(b) Training

Training is the process of **developing skills, habits, and attitudes** through practice and repetition. It is generally **vocational and skill-oriented**.

Definition:

- **Kilpatrick:** "Training is the development of skills, habits, and aptitudes."

Example: Learning computer programming, tailoring, or playing a musical instrument.

(c) Education

Education is the **broadest term** among the three. It is a **life-long, holistic process** that includes knowledge (Gyan), wisdom (Vidya), values, skills, and personality development.

Definitions:

1. **Mahatma Gandhi:** "True education is that which draws out the best in child and man – body, mind, and spirit."
2. **John Dewey:** "Education is the continuous reconstruction of experience."

Example: An individual becoming a responsible citizen through academic knowledge, moral guidance, and skill development.

5. Comparative Table: Teaching, Training, and Education

Basis	Teaching	Training	Education
Focus	Knowledge and facts	Skills and competencies	All-round development (cognitive, social, moral)
Nature	Informative and theoretical	Practical and skill-based	Comprehensive (knowledge + skills + values)
Scope	Limited to	Limited to a	Life-long, universal

	classroom or subject	profession or activity	process
Objective	To give information	To develop efficiency and habits	To build a complete personality
Example	Teaching mathematics	Training in carpentry	Preparing a person to live as a responsible human

6. Relationship between Vidya, Gyan, Teaching, Training, and Education

These five concepts are **interconnected**:

- **Vidya** is the ultimate aim of education.
- **Gyan** is the foundation of Vidya.
- **Teaching** is the means to deliver Gyan.
- **Training** develops practical skills for life.
- **Education** is the holistic process that integrates all the above.

Education (Holistic Development)

│
├── Vidya → Wisdom, higher realization
├── Gyan → Knowledge, facts, information
├── Teaching → Classroom knowledge transfer
└── Training → Practical skill development

7. Modern Perspective

In the **21st century**, the balance between knowledge, wisdom, teaching, and training has become crucial.

- **NEP 2020 (National Education Policy)** emphasizes:
    - Knowledge (academic learning)
    - Skills (training for employability)
    - Values (Vidya for ethical living)
    - Holistic development (true education)

Thus, education today must integrate **Gyan + Vidya + Teaching + Training** for creating responsible global citizens.

1.4 Factors of Education

1. Introduction

Education is not a one-sided process. It is an interaction between different elements that shape the growth and development of an individual. These elements are called the **factors of education**. Without the cooperation of these factors, the aims of education cannot be achieved.

Education involves:

- The **learner** (who receives education)
- The **teacher** (who guides)
- The **curriculum** (the content of learning)
- The **environment** (the surroundings that influence learning)

- The **state/society** (which provides direction and resources)

2. Major Factors of Education

(a) The Child / Learner

- The **child is the central figure** in education.
- Education must suit the child's needs, interests, capacities, and stage of development.
- Modern education is **child-centered** rather than **teacher-centered**.

Quotations:

- **M. K. Gandhi:** "By education I mean an all-round drawing out of the best in child and man – body, mind and spirit."
- **John Dewey:** "The child is the starting point, the center, and the end."

(b) The Teacher

- Teacher plays the role of a **guide, philosopher, and friend**.
- He/she inspires, motivates, and leads the learner towards knowledge and wisdom.
- A good teacher not only imparts knowledge but also inculcates values.

Swami Vivekananda: "The true teacher is he who can immediately come down to the level of the student and transfer his soul to the student's soul."

(c) The Curriculum

- Curriculum is the **total learning experience** provided to students inside or outside the classroom.
- It includes subjects, co-curricular activities, and practical experiences.
- A good curriculum is:
    - Child-centered
    - Flexible
    - Balanced (knowledge, values, and skills)

(d) The Environment

- Education is highly influenced by the environment in which the learner lives.
- **Natural environment** (geography, climate, resources) and **social environment** (family, peer group, culture, media) both shape learning.
- Example: A child growing in a scientific atmosphere becomes more logical and rational.

(e) The State / Society

- The state is responsible for providing **educational facilities and policies**.
- Society decides the **aims of education** according to its cultural, economic, and political needs.
- Example: In democratic societies, education aims to develop democratic values like equality, freedom, and fraternity.

3. Minor Factors (Supporting Elements)

Apart from the major factors, there are some **supporting factors**:

- **Educational Administration** – ensures organization and supervision.
- **Parents and Family** – provide emotional and financial support.
- **Technology** – acts as a modern tool of education.

4. Comparative Table of Major Factors

Factor	Role in Education
Child	Central element, education must suit individual needs
Teacher	Guide, motivator, facilitator of knowledge
Curriculum	Provides content and learning experiences
Environment	Shapes personality through natural and social influences
State/Society	Provides direction, resources, and policies for education

5. Relationship of Factors

All these factors are interdependent. For example:

- Without a learner, there is no education.
- Without a teacher, knowledge transfer is incomplete.

- Without curriculum, learning becomes directionless.
- Without environment, learning cannot be contextual.
- Without state/society, education lacks support and purpose.

6. Conclusion

The factors of education form the **foundation of the teaching-learning process**. A balance among child, teacher, curriculum, environment, and state is essential for achieving the aims of education. Modern education emphasizes **integration of these factors** to provide holistic development of learners.

1.5 Aims of Education – Individual, Social, Democratic, and Vocational

Education is a continuous process of human development, aimed at the holistic growth of individuals and societies. The term "education" encompasses not only formal schooling but also informal and non-formal learning experiences that contribute to the intellectual, emotional, social, and moral development of human beings. One of the most significant questions in educational philosophy is: *What should be the aims of education?* Educational aims provide direction and purpose to the teaching-learning process and determine the outcomes expected from learners. These aims can be broadly classified into **individual, social, democratic, and vocational objectives**.

1. Individual Aims of Education

The individual aim of education emphasizes the development of each person's unique potential. It recognizes the learner as a distinct individual with innate capacities, interests, and abilities. Philosophers and educationists have long advocated for education that nurtures the intellectual, emotional, physical, and moral faculties of individuals.

1.1 Intellectual Development

Education should cultivate the cognitive abilities of learners, including reasoning, critical thinking, problem-solving, and creativity. Intellectual development enables individuals to understand the world, make informed decisions, and contribute meaningfully to society. According to **John Dewey**, education is not merely the transmission of knowledge but a process of developing the ability to think, inquire, and apply knowledge in real-life situations.

1.2 Emotional and Moral Development

Education aims to cultivate emotional intelligence and moral values in individuals. This includes fostering empathy, self-discipline, honesty, and respect for others. **Rousseau**, in his seminal work *Emile*, emphasized that education should nurture the moral and emotional capacities of the child alongside intellectual growth, creating a balanced personality.

1.3 Physical Development

Education also seeks to develop the physical well-being of learners. Physical education, sports, yoga, and health awareness contribute to overall physical fitness, stamina, and discipline. An educated individual must be physically capable to face the challenges of life and perform both personal and societal roles effectively.

1.4 Self-Realization and Personal Growth

An essential aim of education is to enable self-realization. Each individual has latent potential, talents, and abilities. Education should provide opportunities for self-expression, creativity, and personal growth, helping learners achieve their full potential. Indian philosopher **Swami Vivekananda** stressed that education should strengthen character, expand the mind, and awaken the innate divinity within individuals.

Significance: The individual aim of education emphasizes personal autonomy, self-confidence, and lifelong learning. It ensures that learners become responsible, self-reliant, and capable of making meaningful contributions to society.

2. Social Aims of Education

While individual development is crucial, education also has a broader responsibility to society. Social aims of education emphasize preparing individuals to live harmoniously within a community, contribute to social welfare, and participate in cultural and civic life.

2.1 Promoting Social Values and Ethics

Education instills social values such as cooperation, tolerance, justice, and equality. These values enable individuals to interact positively with others and foster a sense of community. **Plato**, in *The Republic*, highlighted the role of education in creating citizens who are morally upright and socially responsible.

2.2 Cultural Transmission

Education serves as a vehicle for transmitting cultural heritage from one generation to another. It introduces learners to languages, traditions, arts, literature, and history, ensuring the continuity of culture and the preservation of societal identity.

2.3 Social Integration

Modern societies are pluralistic, consisting of individuals from diverse backgrounds, religions, and languages. Education helps in promoting social cohesion by teaching respect for diversity and encouraging mutual understanding. **Durkheim**, a prominent sociologist, emphasized that education is fundamental for social integration, as it teaches shared norms, values, and responsibilities.

2.4 Social Responsibility and Civic Awareness

Education aims to prepare individuals to actively contribute to societal welfare. This includes awareness of social issues such as poverty, inequality, environmental conservation, and human rights. Socially aware individuals can participate in community development, volunteerism, and policy-making to promote societal progress.

Significance: Social aims ensure that education produces not only knowledgeable individuals but also socially responsible citizens who can contribute to the harmony, stability, and progress of society.

3. Democratic Aims of Education

In democratic societies, education plays a vital role in fostering democratic values, ensuring equality, and preparing citizens for active participation in governance and decision-making processes.

3.1 Equality of Opportunity

Democratic education promotes equal access to learning for all, irrespective of caste, creed, gender, or socio-economic status. It seeks to reduce disparities and create an inclusive educational system. **Mahatma Gandhi** advocated for education that empowers marginalized communities and provides opportunities for all sections of society.

3.2 Developing Critical Thinking

A democratic society requires citizens capable of independent thought, rational judgment, and informed decision-making. Education encourages critical thinking, debate, and dialogue, enabling individuals to question injustice, challenge prejudice, and uphold democratic principles.

3.3 Encouraging Participation and Citizenship

Education prepares individuals to participate actively in civic life, including voting, public discourse, and community engagement. It fosters a sense of responsibility, rights awareness, and ethical participation in democracy. **Thomas Jefferson** emphasized that an educated citizenry is essential for the survival and flourishing of democracy.

3.4 Promoting Freedom and Tolerance

Democratic education emphasizes freedom of expression, tolerance, and respect for diversity. It teaches learners to appreciate differing viewpoints, resolve conflicts peacefully, and uphold the principles of justice and liberty.

Significance: Democratic aims of education ensure that citizens are informed, responsible, and capable of sustaining democratic institutions. Such education strengthens the political and ethical foundations of society.

4. Vocational Aims of Education

Education is not limited to intellectual, social, or moral development; it also equips individuals with skills necessary for livelihood and professional competence. Vocational aims focus on preparing learners for employment, entrepreneurship, and economic self-reliance.

4.1 Skill Development

Education should provide technical, practical, and professional skills relevant to the changing demands of the labor market. Vocational training programs, internships, and skill-based curricula enable learners to acquire expertise and apply knowledge in real-world scenarios.

4.2 Economic Independence

A vocationally-oriented education equips individuals with the means to earn a livelihood, ensuring economic self-sufficiency and reducing dependency. It fosters entrepreneurship, innovation, and employability, which are essential for personal and national development.

4.3 Bridging Theory and Practice

Vocational education integrates theoretical knowledge with practical application. Students learn to solve problems, adapt to workplace environments, and meet industry standards. This enhances productivity, efficiency, and adaptability.

4.4 Lifelong Career Learning

Vocational aims encourage continuous learning and skill upgrading, allowing individuals to adapt to technological advancements and evolving professions. In today's dynamic world, lifelong learning is crucial for maintaining employability and personal growth.

Significance: Vocational education empowers learners economically and socially, contributing to national development by creating a skilled and competent workforce.

5. Integration of Aims in Modern Education

The four aims of education—individual, social, democratic, and vocational—are interconnected and complementary. A holistic educational system seeks to balance these objectives, ensuring the development of well-rounded individuals who are intellectually competent, morally responsible, socially aware, economically skilled, and democratically engaged.

5.1 Contemporary Educational Perspectives

Modern educational thinkers advocate for a **learner-centered approach** where personal growth, social responsibility, and skill acquisition are integrated into the curriculum. **Howard Gardner's theory of multiple intelligences** supports the development of varied abilities—cognitive, social, and vocational—reflecting the holistic aim of education.

5.2 Challenges and Opportunities

While these aims are universally recognized, implementing them effectively poses challenges. Issues such as unequal access, outdated curricula, insufficient teacher training, and socio-economic disparities hinder the realization of educational goals. Leveraging technology, innovative teaching methods, and policy reforms can enhance the effectiveness of education in achieving its aims.

Chapter 2

Functions of Education

Education is a fundamental tool for shaping individuals and societies. Beyond the acquisition of knowledge, education plays a vital role in **personal and social development**. It equips individuals with the necessary intellectual, emotional, moral, and social competencies to lead meaningful lives and contribute positively to society. The functions of education can broadly be categorized into **personal development**, which focuses on the growth of the individual, and **social development**, which emphasizes societal welfare and cohesion.

1. Personal Development

Personal development refers to the process by which an individual grows intellectually, emotionally, morally, and physically. Education facilitates self-realization, develops critical skills, and enhances the overall personality of the learner.

1.1 Intellectual Development

Education fosters intellectual growth by developing cognitive abilities such as reasoning, problem-solving, critical thinking, and creativity. Intellectual development enables individuals to understand complex concepts, make informed decisions, and innovate.

- **Critical Thinking:** Through education, learners learn to analyze information, question assumptions, and evaluate evidence, which cultivates independent thinking.
- **Problem-Solving Skills:** Education encourages learners to identify problems, explore solutions, and apply knowledge in practical situations.
- **Creativity and Innovation:** Creative thinking is nurtured through arts, literature, science, and project-based learning, allowing individuals to generate novel ideas and solutions.

Example: A student learning science not only memorizes facts but also understands scientific methods, formulates hypotheses, and conducts experiments to derive conclusions.

1.2 Emotional and Moral Development

Education plays a crucial role in shaping emotional intelligence and moral values. Emotional development includes understanding and managing one's emotions, developing empathy, and building positive relationships. Moral development involves understanding the difference between right and wrong and internalizing ethical principles.

- **Empathy and Compassion:** Education helps learners appreciate others' feelings and experiences, fostering kindness and cooperation.
- **Ethical Awareness:** Lessons in history, literature, and philosophy instill moral reasoning and social responsibility.

- **Character Building:** Schools and institutions encourage honesty, self-discipline, perseverance, and integrity through curricula and co-curricular activities.

Example: Participation in group activities, debates, or community service programs helps learners develop interpersonal skills and ethical awareness.

1.3 Physical Development

Physical education is an essential component of personal development. Education promotes health awareness, physical fitness, and coordination. Physical development is necessary for overall well-being and productivity.

- **Health Awareness:** Education provides knowledge about nutrition, hygiene, and disease prevention.
- **Fitness and Sports:** Physical education and sports develop endurance, agility, and teamwork.
- **Stress Management:** Physical activities like yoga and meditation help in maintaining mental and emotional balance.

Example: Schools that incorporate sports and yoga programs enable students to lead a healthy lifestyle and develop resilience.

1.4 Self-Realization and Personal Growth

Education supports self-awareness, self-confidence, and self-expression. Personal growth involves discovering one's strengths, talents, and interests.

- **Self-Expression:** Activities like art, music, drama, and writing allow learners to express their individuality.
- **Self-Confidence:** Academic achievements, skill development, and encouragement build confidence.
- **Lifelong Learning:** Education instills curiosity, motivation, and the habit of continuous learning.

Example: A student engaged in project work or research learns to take initiative, overcome challenges, and develop independent thinking.

2. Social Development

While personal development focuses on the individual, social development emphasizes preparing learners to live harmoniously in society and contribute to collective progress. Education shapes social values, promotes cohesion, and develops responsible citizenship.

2.1 Social Values and Ethics

Education fosters social values such as respect, cooperation, tolerance, justice, and responsibility. It guides learners in understanding societal norms and ethical behavior.

- **Respect and Tolerance:** Education promotes understanding and acceptance of cultural, religious, and linguistic diversity.
- **Cooperation and Teamwork:** Group activities and collaborative learning teach learners to work with others effectively.
- **Justice and Responsibility:** Education encourages fairness, accountability, and ethical decision-making in social interactions.

Example: Classroom discussions on social issues like equality, human rights, and environmental protection teach learners to apply ethical reasoning in real-life situations.

2.2 Social Integration

Modern societies are diverse and complex. Education helps integrate individuals from different backgrounds by promoting shared norms, understanding, and social harmony.

- **Cultural Awareness:** Education introduces learners to their own culture and others, fostering respect and appreciation.
- **Community Participation:** Activities such as volunteering, social service, and awareness campaigns encourage engagement with society.
- **Reduction of Social Inequality:** Education empowers marginalized groups, reducing discrimination and promoting social justice.

Example: Government schemes like *Mid-Day Meal* and *Right to Education (RTE)* ensure equitable access, fostering social inclusion.

2.3 Civic Awareness and Responsibility

Education prepares learners for active citizenship by imparting knowledge about civic rights, duties, and democratic values.

- **Democratic Participation:** Education enables individuals to vote, participate in debates, and understand governance.
- **Social Responsibility:** Learners are encouraged to contribute to societal welfare through initiatives like cleanliness drives, tree plantations, and literacy campaigns.
- **Problem-Solving in Society:** Education equips learners to address social challenges like poverty, environmental degradation, and inequality.

Example: Participation in *National Service Scheme (NSS)* activities helps students understand civic duties and societal responsibilities.

2.4 Promotion of Social Cohesion

Education nurtures a sense of belonging and unity among citizens. Social cohesion is essential for national development and peace.

- **Conflict Resolution:** Education teaches peaceful ways to resolve disputes and understand different perspectives.
- **Social Harmony:** Programs promoting interfaith dialogue, cultural exchange, and community engagement enhance mutual respect.
- **National Identity:** Education helps learners develop pride in their country while respecting global diversity.

Example: Social studies and history lessons that highlight constitutional values, freedom struggles, and democratic ideals foster national unity.

3. Interrelation of Personal and Social Development

Personal and social development are deeply interconnected. A well-developed individual contributes positively to society, and a cohesive society nurtures the growth of its members.

- **Mutual Reinforcement:** Personal growth, such as self-confidence and ethical awareness, supports social participation. Likewise, social experiences, cooperation, and civic engagement enhance personal development.
- **Holistic Education:** Modern educational approaches, such as experiential learning, project-based learning, and community service, integrate personal and social development.
- **Global Perspective:** In an increasingly interconnected world, education emphasizes global citizenship, empathy, and social responsibility, combining personal values with social consciousness.

Example: Students involved in international exchange programs or environmental campaigns develop personal skills and contribute to global social welfare simultaneously.

4. Contemporary Perspectives

Modern educational theorists emphasize that the **primary function of education is holistic development**. Approaches like *constructivist learning*, *collaborative learning*, and *experiential education* focus on both personal and social development.

- **Constructivist Approach:** Encourages learners to construct knowledge through experience, reflection, and social interaction.
- **Multiple Intelligences Theory:** Howard Gardner's framework recognizes varied talents—interpersonal, intrapersonal, linguistic, logical-mathematical, and bodily-kinesthetic—integrating personal and social growth.
- **21st Century Skills:** Critical thinking, creativity, communication, collaboration, and ethical reasoning are emphasized to prepare learners for personal success and societal contribution.

Transmission of Cultural Heritage

Education is not merely the process of imparting knowledge or skills; it is also a **vital instrument for preserving, transmitting, and enriching the cultural heritage of a society**. Culture represents the accumulated knowledge, values, beliefs, traditions, customs, language, art, literature, and social norms of a community. Through education, societies ensure that each generation understands, appreciates, and continues the cultural legacy of their ancestors.

1. Meaning and Significance of Cultural Heritage

Cultural heritage refers to the inherited customs, knowledge, values, art forms, literature, and practices passed down from one generation to the next. It encompasses both tangible heritage (monuments, artifacts, manuscripts) and intangible heritage (language, folklore, rituals, moral values, performing arts).

The **transmission of cultural heritage** through education ensures:

- **Continuity of traditions:** It prevents the loss of cultural identity.
- **Identity formation:** It helps individuals understand their roots and develop a sense of belonging.
- **Moral and ethical development:** Cultural norms and values guide ethical behavior and social conduct.
- **Social cohesion:** Shared cultural knowledge fosters unity and mutual respect among citizens.

Philosophers like **John Dewey** emphasized that education should connect learners with the wisdom of past generations while preparing them for the challenges of modern life. Similarly, **Rabindranath Tagore** advocated education that nurtures both individuality and cultural consciousness.

2. Role of Education in Cultural Transmission

Education plays a multifaceted role in transmitting cultural heritage:

2.1 Language and Literature

Language is the primary medium through which culture is communicated. Literature reflects the values, history, philosophy, and imagination of a society.

- Schools teach native and classical languages to help learners access literary heritage.
- Texts in literature, poetry, and folklore convey cultural narratives, traditions, and moral lessons.
- Bilingual or multilingual education fosters understanding of local and global cultures.

Example: In India, teaching Sanskrit, Hindi, or regional languages in schools helps students connect with ancient texts like the Vedas, epics, and regional literary works.

2.2 Arts, Music, and Performing Traditions

Education introduces students to visual arts, music, dance, and theatre, which are integral aspects of cultural heritage.

- Traditional art forms convey historical, religious, and social values.
- Music and dance serve as mediums for emotional expression and storytelling.
- Schools and cultural institutions organize performances, workshops, and exhibitions to keep traditions alive.

Example: Bharatanatyam, Kathak, and folk music are taught in schools and colleges to preserve India's rich performing arts heritage.

2.3 History and Social Studies

History education ensures learners understand the evolution of their society, significant events, heroes, and movements.

- It fosters national pride and a sense of shared identity.
- Understanding past achievements and struggles helps students appreciate cultural resilience and diversity.
- Social studies impart knowledge of laws, ethics, governance, and societal norms.

Example: Teaching about the Indian freedom struggle, ancient civilizations, and regional histories connects learners to their cultural roots.

2.4 Values, Ethics, and Moral Traditions

Education transmits cultural values and moral principles that guide human behavior.

- Stories, proverbs, rituals, and religious teachings often carry ethical lessons.
- Schools incorporate value education, life skills, and moral instruction to instill respect, honesty, and compassion.
- Cultural heritage reinforces social responsibility and community ethics.

Example: Lessons from the Mahabharata or Panchatantra convey timeless moral principles such as truthfulness, courage, and cooperation.

2.5 Rituals, Customs, and Social Practices

Education familiarizes learners with societal norms, festivals, ceremonies, and customs that shape community life.

- This helps in sustaining local traditions and respecting diversity.
- Understanding cultural practices promotes tolerance and social harmony.

Example: School programs celebrating Diwali, Holi, Eid, Christmas, and regional festivals teach students about pluralism and cultural respect.

3. Methods of Cultural Transmission through Education

The transmission of cultural heritage is achieved through formal, non-formal, and informal educational methods:

3.1 Formal Education

- Curriculum-based learning in schools and colleges includes language, literature, history, arts, and moral education.
- Textbooks, structured lessons, and examinations ensure systematic cultural knowledge dissemination.

3.2 Non-Formal Education

- Workshops, cultural clubs, art classes, and community programs help learners engage actively with culture.
- Museums, heritage centers, and libraries serve as repositories of knowledge and experiences.

3.3 Informal Education

- Family, community, and peer interactions transmit language, customs, and moral values.
- Storytelling, folk songs, and participatory traditions educate individuals in practical cultural norms.

Example: Folk tales narrated by elders in rural communities preserve local history, morals, and traditions.

4. Contemporary Challenges and Opportunities

4.1 Challenges

- **Globalization and Westernization:** Rapid cultural changes threaten traditional knowledge and practices.
- **Technological Distraction:** Excessive digital exposure reduces engagement with local heritage.
- **Urbanization:** Migration to cities often leads to dilution of community-based cultural practices.

4.2 Opportunities

- **Integration of ICT:** Digital archives, virtual museums, and online courses make cultural learning accessible.
- **Curriculum Reforms:** Incorporating local arts, history, and traditions in the curriculum strengthens cultural identity.
- **Intercultural Education:** Encouraging learning about other cultures promotes tolerance and global awareness while preserving local heritage.

5. Significance of Cultural Transmission

The transmission of cultural heritage through education is vital for:

1. **Preservation of Identity:** Helps individuals and communities retain a sense of belonging and pride.
2. **Social Cohesion:** Shared cultural knowledge unites citizens, fostering harmony.
3. **Moral Guidance:** Cultural values provide ethical frameworks for behavior.
4. **Continuity and Innovation:** While preserving tradition, education also inspires creative reinterpretation and adaptation of cultural knowledge.
5. **Global Understanding:** Awareness of one's culture alongside global cultures promotes intercultural dialogue and mutual respect.

Example: Students learning traditional crafts or languages not only preserve heritage but also innovate by blending modern techniques, contributing to cultural sustainability and economic development.

Skill Acquisition in Education

Skill acquisition is one of the central functions of education, aiming to equip learners with the abilities required to perform tasks efficiently, solve problems, and adapt to societal and occupational demands. Education is not limited to theoretical knowledge; it also focuses on the development of practical and cognitive skills that enable individuals to be competent, productive, and self-reliant.

1. Meaning of Skill Acquisition

Skill acquisition refers to the process by which an individual develops the capability to perform tasks effectively through learning and practice. It involves the integration of knowledge, attitudes, and practice to master both **cognitive and practical competencies**.

- Education facilitates the acquisition of intellectual, technical, vocational, and life skills.
- Skills are not innate; they are learned, refined, and applied through continuous practice and feedback.

Example: Learning computer programming involves acquiring the skill to write, debug, and implement code to solve real-world problems.

2. Types of Skills

Education promotes the acquisition of a variety of skills, which can broadly be categorized as follows:

2.1 Cognitive Skills

Cognitive skills involve the mental processes of thinking, reasoning, problem-solving, and decision-making.

- **Critical Thinking:** The ability to analyze, evaluate, and synthesize information.
- **Problem-Solving:** Identifying challenges and applying knowledge to find solutions.
- **Creativity and Innovation:** Developing new ideas or approaches.

Example: A science student using analytical reasoning to conduct experiments demonstrates cognitive skill development.

2.2 Technical and Vocational Skills

Technical skills involve specific practical abilities required to perform a profession or occupation.

- **Vocational Training:** Skills in areas such as carpentry, plumbing, electrical work, tailoring, or agriculture.
- **Digital and Technological Skills:** Proficiency in computers, software applications, and digital tools.

Example: A student trained in graphic design learns to use software tools to create professional-quality digital content.

2.3 Social and Interpersonal Skills

Social skills enable effective communication, collaboration, and relationship-building.

- **Communication Skills:** Writing, speaking, and listening effectively.
- **Teamwork:** Cooperating with peers to achieve common goals.
- **Leadership and Negotiation:** Guiding groups and resolving conflicts constructively.

Example: Group projects in school or college enhance collaborative problem-solving and leadership skills.

2.4 Life Skills

Life skills are essential for personal development and coping with everyday challenges.

- **Decision-Making and Goal-Setting:** Planning and making informed choices.
- **Time Management:** Organizing tasks efficiently to meet deadlines.
- **Adaptability and Resilience:** Adjusting to changes and overcoming setbacks.

Example: Workshops on stress management and career planning equip students with skills to navigate personal and professional life effectively.

3. Methods of Skill Acquisition

Education employs various methods to facilitate skill acquisition:

3.1 Experiential Learning

- Learning by doing enhances understanding and retention.
- Activities like laboratory experiments, internships, and fieldwork develop practical skills.

Example: Engineering students gain technical proficiency through hands-on lab work.

3.2 Project-Based Learning

- Students work on real-world projects to apply knowledge creatively.
- Encourages problem-solving, collaboration, and innovation.

Example: Developing a community awareness campaign teaches research, communication, and organizational skills.

3.3 Vocational Training and Apprenticeships

- Structured training in a specific trade or profession provides specialized skills.
- Combines classroom instruction with practical experience.

Example: An apprentice electrician acquires technical skills by working under an experienced professional.

3.4 Use of Technology

- Digital tools and online platforms enable skill development through simulations, tutorials, and virtual practice.
- Online coding platforms, virtual labs, and interactive software support cognitive and technical skill acquisition.

Example: Learning artificial intelligence programming through online platforms develops both technical and problem-solving skills.

3.5 Collaborative and Peer Learning

- Group discussions, teamwork, and peer teaching enhance interpersonal and social skills.
- Collaborative learning encourages sharing of knowledge and collective problem-solving.

Example: Students working together on a science project learn communication, coordination, and decision-making skills.

4. Importance of Skill Acquisition

Skill acquisition is essential for individual, societal, and economic development.

4.1 Personal Empowerment

- Equips individuals with the ability to perform tasks competently.
- Enhances self-confidence, independence, and employability.

Example: A student skilled in coding or digital marketing can pursue freelance opportunities or entrepreneurship.

4.2 Economic and Vocational Relevance

- Skills are directly linked to employability and productivity.
- Vocational skills reduce unemployment and support economic growth.

Example: Skilled artisans, technicians, and IT professionals contribute to industry and commerce.

4.3 Social and Civic Contribution

- Skills enable individuals to contribute effectively to society.
- Enhances problem-solving and innovation in community development projects.

Example: Life skills like communication, conflict resolution, and leadership help in organizing social initiatives and awareness programs.

4.4 Lifelong Learning

- Skill acquisition encourages continuous learning and adaptability.
- In a rapidly changing world, new skills are constantly needed to stay relevant.

Example: Professionals updating digital or AI-related skills demonstrate adaptability and ongoing personal growth.

5. Educational Theories Supporting Skill Acquisition

- **John Dewey's Experiential Learning Theory:** Emphasizes "learning by doing" to develop practical and cognitive skills.
- **Constructivist Theory (Piaget & Vygotsky):** Learners actively construct knowledge through experience and social interaction.
- **Multiple Intelligences Theory (Howard Gardner):** Recognizes diverse abilities (linguistic, logical, bodily-kinesthetic, interpersonal) and promotes varied skill development.

6. Challenges in Skill Acquisition

- **Outdated Curricula:** Traditional education often emphasizes theory over practical skills.
- **Resource Limitations:** Lack of labs, tools, or vocational training centers hampers skill development.
- **Teacher Preparedness:** Educators require training in modern teaching methods and skill-oriented pedagogy.
- **Digital Divide:** Limited access to technology restricts acquisition of 21st-century skills.

Solution: Curriculum reforms, experiential learning, vocational programs, and technology integration can enhance skill acquisition effectively.

Acquisition and Creation of Human Values

Education is not merely the transmission of knowledge or development of skills; it also plays a pivotal role in the **acquisition and creation of human values**. Human values are the principles, ethics, and standards that guide individual behavior and social interaction. They encompass moral, cultural, spiritual, and civic dimensions, helping individuals lead meaningful lives and contribute positively to society.

1. Meaning of Human Values

Human values refer to fundamental beliefs and ethical principles that govern human conduct. They include values such as honesty, compassion, tolerance, justice, empathy, respect, responsibility, and integrity. Values guide decisions, shape behavior, and establish norms for personal and social life.

- **Acquisition of values** involves learning and internalizing societal, cultural, and ethical norms.
- **Creation of values** refers to the ability of individuals to reflect, innovate, and adapt values to address contemporary challenges and unique life situations.

Philosophers like **Mahatma Gandhi** emphasized that education should cultivate moral and spiritual values alongside intellectual growth, shaping responsible citizens and compassionate human beings.

2. Acquisition of Human Values through Education

The acquisition of human values is a process where learners internalize the ethical and moral principles prevalent in society. Education facilitates this in several ways:

2.1 Moral Education

- Formal teaching of ethics, philosophy, and moral stories helps learners understand right and wrong.
- Discussion of moral dilemmas enhances ethical reasoning and judgment.

Example: Stories from Indian epics like the *Ramayana* and *Mahabharata* teach honesty, courage, and duty.

2.2 Value-Based Curriculum

- Integrating value education in subjects like social studies, literature, and environmental studies reinforces principles such as equality, justice, and social responsibility.
- Schools often conduct workshops, debates, and awareness campaigns to embed values in learners' daily lives.

Example: Lessons on human rights, civic duties, and environmental conservation instill responsibility and empathy.

2.3 Role of Teachers and Mentors

- Teachers act as role models, demonstrating values through their behavior, interactions, and pedagogy.
- Mentorship and guidance help students internalize values through observation and reflection.

Example: A teacher who emphasizes cooperation and fairness in classroom activities encourages students to adopt similar values.

2.4 Social and Cultural Exposure

- Participation in community service, cultural programs, and cooperative learning fosters empathy, respect, and social awareness.
- Exposure to diverse cultures and communities enhances tolerance and understanding.

Example: Students volunteering in social service projects learn compassion and civic responsibility.

2.5 Reflection and Experiential Learning

- Learners acquire values by reflecting on their experiences and understanding the consequences of their actions.
- Experiential learning, including role-playing and service-learning, strengthens moral understanding.

Example: Participating in environmental clean-up drives helps learners internalize environmental responsibility.

3. Creation of Human Values

While acquisition involves learning existing values, education also encourages the **creation of new values**. This is particularly important in a rapidly changing world where traditional norms may need adaptation.

3.1 Critical Thinking and Ethical Reflection

- Learners are encouraged to question existing norms and evaluate ethical principles critically.
- Reflection and reasoning help in creating values that are relevant, just, and humane.

Example: Students analyzing contemporary ethical issues like AI ethics or climate justice develop innovative approaches to human values.

3.2 Cultural and Artistic Innovation

- Through arts, literature, and creative expression, learners can explore new perspectives on human experience.
- Education encourages reinterpretation of traditional values in contemporary contexts.

Example: Literature or theatre projects addressing gender equality promote new social values while respecting cultural heritage.

3.3 Social Experimentation and Civic Engagement

- Participating in social initiatives, volunteer work, and policy advocacy allows learners to develop values that respond to real-world challenges.
- Active citizenship encourages the creation of values that promote justice, equality, and sustainability.

Example: Students initiating awareness campaigns on mental health create a culture of empathy and understanding.

3.4 Integration of Global Perspectives

- Education exposes learners to global challenges, diverse cultures, and international human rights principles.
- This exposure helps students create universal values such as tolerance, equity, and environmental stewardship.

Example: Programs on global citizenship education encourage the creation of values that balance local traditions with global responsibilities.

4. Importance of Human Values in Education

4.1 Personal Development

- Human values shape character, build self-discipline, and promote emotional intelligence.
- They guide individuals to make ethical decisions and lead meaningful lives.

4.2 Social Harmony

- Values such as respect, tolerance, and cooperation ensure peaceful coexistence in diverse societies.
- Education fosters civic responsibility and social cohesion.

4.3 Ethical Leadership and Responsible Citizenship

- Value-based education cultivates leaders who are ethical, just, and socially responsible.
- Citizens guided by human values participate actively in democratic governance and community welfare.

4.4 Adaptation to Contemporary Challenges

- The creation of new values enables societies to address evolving issues like technological ethics, environmental conservation, and social justice.
- Education ensures that human values remain relevant and actionable.

5. Educational Approaches for Values

- **Integrated Curriculum:** Incorporating values across subjects rather than teaching them separately.
- **Experiential Learning:** Encouraging learning through real-life experiences, projects, and service.
- **Collaborative Learning:** Peer discussions, debates, and teamwork enhance understanding of diverse perspectives.

- **Role Modeling:** Teachers, mentors, and community leaders exemplify ethical behavior.
- **Reflection and Dialogue:** Encouraging learners to reflect on personal experiences and societal issues.

6. Challenges in Acquiring and Creating Human Values

- **Cultural Conflicts:** Conflicting societal values may confuse learners.
- **Technological Influence:** Social media and digital culture can sometimes promote superficial or materialistic values.
- **Neglect in Curriculum:** Overemphasis on academic achievement may reduce focus on ethical and moral education.
- **Globalization:** Rapid change requires adaptation of traditional values to modern contexts.

Solution: Holistic education, experiential learning, and value-integrated curricula can address these challenges effectively.

2.5: Social Cohesion

1. Introduction

Education is not only a process of acquiring knowledge but also a powerful tool for creating unity among people. In society, different individuals live together with diverse backgrounds, languages, religions, and cultures. For peaceful living, there must be **social**

cohesion. Education plays a vital role in bringing individuals closer, reducing conflicts, and developing a sense of belongingness.

This section explains the **meaning, definitions, nature, and importance of social cohesion**, and how education contributes to it.

2. Meaning of Social Cohesion

The word *cohesion* means *to stick together*. Thus, **social cohesion** means the **bonding and unity among members of a society**. It refers to the way people accept each other, cooperate, and live in harmony despite differences.

- In simple words: **Social cohesion means unity, trust, and cooperation among people in a society.**

Key Elements:

- Trust among individuals and groups.
- Respect for diversity.
- Shared values and culture.
- Cooperation for common goals.
- Peaceful conflict resolution.

3. Definitions of Social Cohesion

Different thinkers and institutions have defined social cohesion in their own ways.

Scholar/Institution	Definition

Durkheim (1893)	Social cohesion is the force that binds individuals together in society through shared values and collective conscience.
OECD (2011)	A cohesive society is one that works towards the well-being of all its members, fights exclusion and marginalisation, and creates a sense of belonging.
Council of Europe (2008)	Social cohesion is the capacity of a society to ensure the welfare of all its members, minimise disparities, and avoid polarisation.
UNESCO	Social cohesion means living together with mutual respect, tolerance, and peaceful coexistence in diversity.

4. Nature of Social Cohesion

The nature of social cohesion can be understood through the following points:

1. **Integrative** – It integrates people from different sections of society.
2. **Dynamic** – It keeps changing with time and situations.
3. **Value-based** – It depends on respect, tolerance, and equality.
4. **Inclusive** – It includes every group irrespective of caste, class, gender, or religion.
5. **Educational** – It can be developed through proper teaching and learning processes.

5. Importance of Social Cohesion in Education

Education is one of the strongest means of building social cohesion.

Aspect	Contribution of Education
National Unity	Develops respect for the nation, constitution, and democratic values.
Peaceful Living	Reduces conflicts through teaching tolerance and mutual respect.
Social Equality	Promotes equality and justice in classrooms and society.
Cultural Integration	Encourages appreciation of diverse languages, traditions, and lifestyles.
Global Citizenship	Prepares students to respect international cooperation and peace.

6. Functions of Education in Promoting Social Cohesion

Education contributes to social cohesion in many ways:

(a) Transmission of Common Values

Schools transmit social, moral, and cultural values to children, which create unity.

(b) Development of Democratic Spirit

Through democratic classroom practices, students learn equality, justice, and participation.

(c) Promotion of Tolerance

Education helps in respecting different religions, languages, and traditions.

(d) Reducing Social Conflicts

When students learn about peace, human rights, and cooperation, social conflicts reduce.

(e) Encouraging Team Work

Group learning, co-curricular activities, and community service bring students together.

7. Barriers to Social Cohesion

Sometimes, education fails to create unity because of certain challenges:

1. **Casteism and Communalism** – Discrimination weakens unity.
2. **Economic Inequality** – Gap between rich and poor creates division.
3. **Gender Discrimination** – Unequal opportunities disturb social balance.
4. **Lack of Value Education** – Without moral education, respect and tolerance decline.
5. **Excessive Competition** – Over-focus on exams reduces cooperation.

8. Social Cohesion and NEP 2020

The **National Education Policy (NEP) 2020** gives special importance to social cohesion.

- Promotes **inclusive and equitable education** for all.
- Focuses on **value-based education** and **constitutional values**.
- Encourages **multilingualism and cultural exchange**.
- Strengthens **gender inclusion fund** and education for disadvantaged groups.
- Promotes **experiential learning, teamwork, and community participation**.

Thus, NEP 2020 makes education a tool for national integration and global harmony.

9. Examples of Social Cohesion through Education

- **Morning Assembly in Schools** – Common prayers, national anthem, and pledge create unity.
- **Celebration of Festivals** – Celebrating Diwali, Eid, Christmas, and other festivals in schools builds respect for all religions.
- **Community Projects** – Students working on cleanliness drives or plantation campaigns develop teamwork.
- **Inclusive Classrooms** – Children of different backgrounds studying together reduce social barriers.

10. Educational Practices for Social Cohesion

Teachers and institutions can apply several methods:

1. **Value Education** – Teaching honesty, equality, cooperation, and compassion.
2. **Peace Education** – Introducing lessons on conflict resolution.
3. **Collaborative Learning** – Group discussions and teamwork activities.
4. **Multicultural Education** – Introducing students to different cultural practices.
5. **Service Learning** – Encouraging participation in community welfare activities.

11. Table: Difference between a Cohesive and Non-Cohesive Society

Cohesive Society	Non-Cohesive Society
Unity and trust	Division and conflict
Equality and justice	Discrimination and inequality
Cooperation	Competition and selfishness
Respect for diversity	Intolerance
Peaceful coexistence	Violence and unrest

2.6 Education for Leisure

1. Introduction

Human life is not only about work and survival. Along with work, people also need **rest, recreation, and creative use of free time**. This free time is called **leisure**. If leisure is not used properly, it can lead to laziness, boredom, and even negative habits. Therefore, **education for leisure** is very important. It trains individuals to use their free time in meaningful, creative, and productive ways.

In the modern age, where technology has reduced working hours, the importance of leisure has increased. Hence, education must prepare students not only for jobs but also for the **right use of leisure**.

2. Meaning of Leisure

- The word **"leisure"** comes from the Latin word *licere* meaning "to be free."
- **Leisure means the free time left after completing essential duties of work, study, and responsibilities.**
- It is not just idleness but an opportunity for **rest, refreshment, self-development, and enjoyment.**

Example:

- Reading a book, painting, playing sports, gardening, or doing social service in free time.

3. Definitions of Leisure

Scholar/Source	Definition

Aristotle	Leisure is the basis of culture, where a person engages in noble activities beyond mere survival.
Dumazedier (French sociologist)	Leisure is a set of occupations in which the individual engages freely after work, for relaxation, amusement, and self-enrichment.
UNESCO	Leisure is the free time which can be used creatively for personal growth and community development.

4. Meaning of Education for Leisure

- **Education for leisure** means training individuals to use their free time in **positive, healthy, and creative ways**.
- It includes developing **hobbies, interests, and values** so that leisure contributes to the growth of personality and society.

In simple words: □ **Education for leisure is the guidance provided by schools, colleges, and society to help people use their free time fruitfully.**

5. Objectives of Education for Leisure

1. To develop **constructive hobbies** like art, music, reading, and sports.
2. To avoid misuse of leisure in harmful activities (addiction, excessive media use).

3. To encourage **social service and community participation**.
4. To promote **physical and mental health**.
5. To help in **emotional balance and stress management**.
6. To prepare students for **lifelong learning** and self-improvement.

6. Importance of Education for Leisure

Education for leisure is important in both **individual life** and **social life**.

Individual Importance	Social Importance
Provides rest and refreshment	Promotes cultural activities
Encourages creativity	Builds community harmony
Improves mental health	Reduces crime and negative habits
Develops personality	Encourages social service
Reduces stress	Promotes national integration

7. Factors Influencing Leisure

1. **Economic Condition** – Wealthy people may have more leisure, but education teaches everyone to use it wisely.
2. **Technology** – Machines and AI reduce work hours, giving more free time.

3. **Culture and Tradition** – Festivals, folk arts, and cultural practices shape leisure activities.
4. **Education** – Schools and universities guide students in developing meaningful hobbies.
5. **Social Media** – Provides new options, but can also waste time if not used carefully.

8. Role of Education in Proper Use of Leisure

Education helps individuals to use leisure in balanced and creative ways:

1. **Physical Activities** – Sports, yoga, and outdoor games.
2. **Artistic Activities** – Music, dance, painting, and drama.
3. **Intellectual Activities** – Reading, writing, debating, online learning.
4. **Social Activities** – Volunteering, community work, cultural programs.
5. **Spiritual Activities** – Meditation, prayer, self-reflection.

9. Educational Practices for Leisure (Examples from Schools/Colleges)

- **Clubs and Societies** – Literary club, music club, debating club.
- **Sports and Games** – Regular physical education periods.
- **Library Use** – Encouraging students to read beyond textbooks.
- **Skill-based Courses** – Art, craft, gardening, computer skills.

- **Community Service** – NSS, NCC, Red Cross activities.

10. Challenges in Education for Leisure

1. **Overuse of Social Media** – Students spend too much time online.
2. **Commercialisation of Leisure** – Expensive hobbies not affordable to all.
3. **Lack of Guidance** – Schools focus only on exams, not leisure training.
4. **Peer Pressure** – Wrong company can lead to misuse of free time.
5. **Addictions** – Drugs, alcohol, or gaming addiction misguide leisure.

11. Education for Leisure and NEP 2020

The **National Education Policy (NEP) 2020** strongly supports education for leisure through:

- **Holistic development** – Arts, sports, and vocational activities along with academics.
- **Skill development** – Hobbies like coding, music, painting, and yoga.
- **Bagless Days** – Encouraging students to engage in arts and community service.
- **Experiential Learning** – Field trips, creative projects, and internships.

- **Value Education** – Promoting discipline, peace, and harmony.

Thus, NEP 2020 aims to make learning enjoyable and ensure that students develop meaningful leisure interests.

12. Examples of Constructive Leisure Activities

Activity	Benefit
Reading books	Expands knowledge and imagination
Playing sports	Improves health and teamwork
Music and dance	Develops creativity and emotional balance
Gardening	Promotes love for nature
Yoga and meditation	Reduces stress and improves focus
Social service	Builds responsibility and empathy

13. Views of Indian Thinkers on Education for Leisure

- **Mahatma Gandhi** – Advocated *Basic Education (Nai Talim)* where work and play were combined, making leisure productive.
- **Rabindranath Tagore** – Emphasised music, art, and nature study as joyful learning and leisure.
- **Swami Vivekananda** – Believed that games, physical exercise, and meditation strengthen body and mind.

- **Dr. Radhakrishnan** – Stressed that education should provide opportunities for both intellectual and cultural enrichment.

2.7 Education for National Integration

1. Introduction

India is a land of great **diversity** – diversity of languages, religions, castes, cultures, and traditions. While this diversity is our strength, it can also create **divisions and conflicts** if not handled properly. To live in peace and progress together, India needs **national integration** – the feeling of unity among all citizens despite differences.

□ **Education is the most powerful instrument to promote national integration.** It helps students to develop respect for diversity, love for the nation, and a spirit of common brotherhood.

2. Meaning of National Integration

- **National integration** means the process of bringing together people of different castes, religions, languages, and regions into one unified nation.
- It is not the loss of diversity, but the **unity in diversity**.

Simple Meaning:

□ *National integration is the feeling that "We are Indians first, before belonging to any caste, religion, or language group."*

3. Definitions of National Integration

Scholar/Source	Definition
Dr. S. Radhakrishnan	National integration is a psychological and educational process to make people feel they are members of one nation.
Kothari Commission (1964-66)	"National integration is the awareness of a common identity among the citizens of a country."
National Integration Council (1961)	It is the development of a sense of unity, solidarity, and loyalty among the people of India.

4. Importance of National Integration

1. **For Unity and Stability** – A united country can face internal and external challenges strongly.
2. **For Democracy** – Democracy works only when citizens respect equality and fraternity.
3. **For Economic Development** – Without unity, no large-scale development is possible.
4. **For Peace and Harmony** – Reduces communalism, casteism, and regionalism.

5. **For Global Identity** – A united India earns respect in the international community.

5. Threats to National Integration

1. **Communalism** – Conflicts between religious communities.
2. **Casteism** – Discrimination and inequality based on caste.
3. **Regionalism** – Excessive attachment to local or regional identity.
4. **Linguistic Differences** – Conflicts over language.
5. **Economic Inequality** – Rich–poor gap creates frustration and division.
6. **Political Manipulation** – Leaders sometimes divide people for vote-bank politics.

6. Role of Education in National Integration

Education plays a key role in promoting unity. It develops values, attitudes, and practices that strengthen national identity.

Ways Education Promotes National Integration

1. **Common Curriculum** – Teaching shared history, culture, and constitutional values.
2. **Value Education** – Respect for equality, tolerance, and secularism.
3. **Language Policy** – Promoting multilingualism and Hindi/English as link languages.

4. **Celebration of Festivals** – Observing national days (Independence Day, Republic Day).
5. **Cultural Exchange** – Student exchange programs across states.
6. **Co-curricular Activities** – NCC, NSS, Scouts, Youth Parliament for national service.
7. **Textbooks and Literature** – Teaching stories of unity, freedom struggle, and Indian heroes.

7. Objectives of Education for National Integration

1. To create **awareness of Indian heritage and culture**.
2. To develop a sense of **pride and loyalty towards the nation**.
3. To reduce social evils like casteism, communalism, and untouchability.
4. To inculcate **constitutional values** – equality, liberty, fraternity, and justice.
5. To promote **social harmony and tolerance**.
6. To encourage students to work for **national development**.

8. Methods of Education for National Integration

1. **Curricular Methods**
    - Inclusion of lessons on freedom fighters, constitution, and cultural unity.
    - Moral and value education.
2. **Co-Curricular Methods**
    - Sports, debates, cultural programs, NCC, NSS.

   - Educational tours and field trips.
3. **Social and Community Methods**
   - Social service camps, blood donation drives.
   - Participation in Swachh Bharat Abhiyan or local development projects.
4. **Use of ICT and Media**
   - Documentaries, films, and digital resources promoting unity.

9. National Policies and Programs for Integration

- **National Policy on Education (1986, updated 1992)** – Emphasized value education and common core curriculum.
- **NEP 2020** – Highlights Indian knowledge systems, cultural diversity, and constitutional values to promote unity.
- **National Integration Council (1961)** – Established to resolve communal and regional conflicts.
- **Ek Bharat Shreshtha Bharat (2015)** – Cultural exchange program between states.
- **NCC and NSS** – Encourage discipline, service, and unity among youth.

10. Thinkers' Views on Education and National Unity

- **Mahatma Gandhi** – Believed in "Sarva Dharma Sambhava" (equal respect for all religions). Education should promote communal harmony.
- **Rabindranath Tagore** – Advocated for internationalism and unity beyond narrow boundaries.

- **Dr. A.P.J. Abdul Kalam** – Stressed that youth should be inspired to think of India first, above all divisions.

11. Table: Barriers vs. Solutions through Education

Barrier to National Integration	Educational Solution
Communalism	Teaching secularism and harmony through curriculum
Casteism	Promoting equality and dignity of all through social justice education
Regionalism	Student exchange programs, interstate cultural festivals
Linguistic conflicts	Promotion of three-language formula and respect for all languages
Economic inequality	Vocational training, skill development, scholarships

12. Case Examples of Education for National Integration

1. **Independence Movement** – Leaders like Gandhi, Nehru, and Patel used education to unite people across regions.
2. **Kendriya Vidyalayas** – Provide uniform education to children of different states and backgrounds.

3. **NCC Camps** – Students from different states live, learn, and train together.
4. **School Celebrations** – Flag hoisting, patriotic songs, and plays create unity.

13. Education for National Integration under NEP 2020

- **Holistic Curriculum** – Focus on Indian traditions, art, music, and philosophy.
- **Ethics and Constitutional Values** – Curriculum includes freedom, equality, fraternity, human rights.
- **Mother Tongue & Multilingualism** – Respect for regional languages, along with link languages.
- **Skill Development** – Reduce economic inequality through vocational education.
- **Inclusive Education** – Promote education of women, marginalized groups, and differently-abled for equality.

2.8: Education for International Understanding

Introduction

The world today is closely interconnected. Modern technology, communication, travel, and trade have reduced distances among nations. Problems such as climate change, terrorism, pandemics, poverty, and wars are not limited to one country but affect the entire world. In this situation, **Education for International Understanding (EIU)** becomes essential. It prepares students to think beyond their nation, respect cultural differences, and contribute to global peace and cooperation.

As the great educator **Mahatma Gandhi** said: *"I do not want my house to be walled in on all sides and my windows to be stuffed. I want the cultures of all lands to be blown about my house as freely as possible."*

This vision is the essence of international understanding through education.

Concept of International Understanding

International understanding means developing in individuals:

- A **sense of world citizenship** beyond narrow nationalism.
- **Respect for diversity** of cultures, religions, and traditions.
- **Tolerance and cooperation** in solving global issues.
- A belief in **peaceful coexistence** and **human unity**.

According to **UNESCO (1974 Recommendation on Education for International Understanding)**: *"Education for international understanding, co-operation and peace should aim to strengthen respect for human rights and fundamental freedoms, develop awareness of interdependence of peoples and nations, and encourage international solidarity."*

Aims of Education for International Understanding

1. **Peace and Harmony** – Promoting peaceful settlement of disputes.
2. **Cultural Exchange** – Understanding and appreciating other cultures.
3. **Global Citizenship** – Developing awareness of global issues.
4. **Human Rights** – Promoting justice, equality, and dignity.
5. **Environmental Awareness** – Recognizing global responsibility for nature.
6. **Economic and Social Cooperation** – Understanding interdependence of nations.

Need for International Understanding in Education

- To prevent **wars and conflicts**.
- To deal with **global challenges** (climate, epidemics, terrorism).
- To develop **tolerance and empathy** in youth.
- To encourage **world brotherhood and peace**.
- To create **responsible global citizens** in the 21st century.

Factors that Promote International Understanding

Factor	Role in International Understanding
Curriculum	Inclusion of world history, geography, global problems.
Language Learning	Encourages communication with people of other nations.

Exchange Programs	Student/teacher exchange develops real cultural contact.
Media & ICT	Provides global news, perspectives, and awareness.
Peace Education	Trains learners in conflict resolution and tolerance.
UN & UNESCO Programs	Promote cultural exchange, human rights, and global education.

Role of Teachers and Schools

1. **Teachers** must encourage open-mindedness, tolerance, and respect for all.
2. **Schools** should celebrate international days (UN Day, Human Rights Day).
3. **Activities** such as debates, projects, and cultural exchange should be organized.
4. Use of **educational technology** to connect students globally (virtual classrooms, online collaborations).

Examples and Stories

- When **World War II** ended, many educators realized that wars begin in the minds of men; therefore, peace must also begin in the minds of men. This led to the establishment of **UNESCO in 1945**, with the aim to promote peace through education, culture, and science.

- **Tagore's Santiniketan** welcomed students from across the world to live and study together, promoting unity in diversity.
- **United Nations programs** like Model UN (MUN) help students practice diplomacy and international cooperation.

Challenges in Implementing International Understanding

1. **Nationalism vs. Globalism** – Sometimes patriotism creates narrow attitudes.
2. **Political Conflicts** – Wars and border disputes affect harmony.
3. **Cultural Misunderstanding** – Lack of proper exposure to other cultures.
4. **Language Barriers** – Communication gaps among people.
5. **Economic Inequality** – Creates differences between developed and developing nations.

Measures to Strengthen International Understanding

- Introducing **peace education and human rights education** in curriculum.
- Organizing **international student exchange programs**.
- Promoting **multilingual education**.
- Using **digital platforms** for cultural sharing.
- Encouraging **world history and global studies** in higher education.

- Strengthening **UNESCO Associated Schools Project (ASPnet)** to promote cultural unity.

2.9 Education for Human Resource Development

Introduction

Education is a vital instrument for individual growth and national development. Among its many purposes, **Human Resource Development (HRD)** stands out as a major goal of modern education. HRD focuses on developing the human capabilities needed for sustainable development and economic progress. It is about equipping people with knowledge, skills, attitudes, and values so they can contribute meaningfully to society and the economy.

In the framework of **NEP 2020**, HRD has become a central theme, aiming to integrate education with skill development and employability, ensuring that learners are prepared for the challenges of the 21st century.

Meaning of Education for Human Resource Development

Human Resource Development is a process of enhancing the abilities and skills of individuals to make them more productive members of society. **Education for HRD** means a planned process of acquiring knowledge, developing skills, and building attitudes to meet the economic, social, and cultural needs of a nation.

Simple Definition: Education for HRD is training individuals to be skilled, knowledgeable, adaptable, and socially responsible so they can contribute to personal growth and national development.

The Concept of Human Resource

Human resources are the people who make up the workforce of a nation. They are not just labour but also the intellectual and creative assets of society. In this sense, **HRD treats education as a continuous investment in people** — a process that enhances their productivity and capacity to innovate.

Importance of Education for Human Resource Development

Education for HRD has far-reaching importance in a developing country like India:

1. **Economic Growth:** Skilled human resources increase productivity, reduce wastage, and enhance competitiveness in national and global markets.
2. **Social Development:** Education promotes social harmony, equality, and the ability to solve social problems.
3. **Technological Advancement:** HRD ensures that the workforce can adapt to and innovate in new technologies.
4. **National Progress:** Strong human capital forms the backbone of national development.
5. **Personal Empowerment:** Education for HRD increases employability, personal income, and quality of life.

Objectives of Education for Human Resource Development

The objectives of HRD through education can be summarised as follows:

1. **Skill Development:** To equip learners with vocational and technical skills required in the job market.
2. **Knowledge Enhancement:** To develop intellectual abilities, critical thinking, and problem-solving skills.
3. **Attitude Formation:** To build positive attitudes such as discipline, cooperation, and adaptability.
4. **Productivity Improvement:** To prepare individuals who can contribute effectively to the economy.
5. **Leadership and Innovation:** To develop leadership qualities and innovative thinking.
6. **Lifelong Learning:** To encourage continuous learning for adapting to changes.
7. **Alignment with National Needs:** To prepare human resources in line with national development plans.

Features of Education for Human Resource Development

Features	Explanation
Skill Development	Focus on vocational and technical skills for employability.
Knowledge Expansion	Enhancing subject knowledge, problem-solving, and critical thinking abilities.

Attitude Formation	Encouraging ethical values, social responsibility, and adaptability.
Continuous Learning	Promoting lifelong learning and skill updating.
Leadership and Innovation	Encouraging creativity and leadership qualities.
Alignment with National Needs	Linking education programs with the country's socio-economic priorities.

Role of Education in HRD

Education plays a central role in developing human resources. Different forms of education contribute to HRD in specific ways:

1. Formal Education

Formal schooling, college, and university education provide foundational knowledge, theoretical understanding, and analytical skills. They also help in shaping attitudes and values essential for productive citizenship.

2. Vocational Education

Vocational education focuses on job-specific training that equips learners with practical skills. It is a key element in NEP 2020, which stresses integrating vocational training from school level onwards.

3. Professional Education

Professional education prepares individuals for specialized careers like medicine, engineering, law, and management. This form of education strengthens expertise and innovation.

4. Lifelong Learning

In a rapidly changing world, continuous learning is vital. HRD requires constant updating of skills and knowledge to keep pace with technological and social changes.

Education for HRD in NEP 2020

The **National Education Policy 2020** emphasises the role of education in developing human capital for national prosperity. Some key features of NEP 2020 in HRD include:

- **Skill Development from School Level:** Vocational courses integrated from Grade 6 onwards.
- **Multidisciplinary Approach:** Linking arts, sciences, and vocational subjects to broaden skills and creativity.
- **Technology Integration:** Use of AI, digital learning, and ICT for skill enhancement.
- **Lifelong Learning Pathways:** Flexible learning structures to allow upskilling throughout life.
- **Focus on Innovation and Research:** Encouraging creativity, innovation, and entrepreneurship.

Challenges in Education for Human Resource Development

While the importance of HRD is widely recognised, some challenges remain:

1. **Quality of Education:** Lack of quality infrastructure and trained teachers.
2. **Mismatch of Skills:** Education not always aligned with industry needs.
3. **Digital Divide:** Unequal access to technology and digital learning tools.
4. **Limited Vocational Integration:** Vocational education is still not widely available at school level.
5. **Brain Drain:** Skilled human resources migrating to other countries.

Addressing these challenges is vital for effective HRD.

Strategies for Effective HRD through Education

To strengthen HRD through education, the following strategies are essential:

1. **Curriculum Reform:** Align education with skills needed in the job market.
2. **Vocational Training:** Integrate skill-based education from early schooling.
3. **Industry Collaboration:** Partnership between education institutions and industries.

4. **Use of Technology:** Expand e-learning and digital resources for skill development.
5. **Teacher Training:** Equip teachers with skills to deliver HRD-focused education.
6. **Promoting Innovation and Entrepreneurship:** Encourage students to think creatively and start ventures.

Conclusion

Education for Human Resource Development is more than the transmission of knowledge—it is a dynamic process of preparing individuals for the demands of the modern world. In a rapidly globalising economy, the quality of human resources determines a nation's progress. NEP 2020 recognises this by integrating vocational education, skill development, technology, and lifelong learning into the education system.

By focusing on HRD, education transforms individuals into skilled, adaptable, innovative, and socially responsible citizens capable of contributing to the sustainable development of the nation.

□ Summary Table — Education for HRD

Aspect	Details
Meaning	Developing human skills, knowledge, and attitudes for productivity.
Importance	Economic growth, social progress, technological advancement, empowerment.

Objectives	Skill development, knowledge enhancement, attitude formation, productivity, leadership, lifelong learning.
Features	Skill focus, knowledge expansion, attitude formation, continuous learning, innovation, national alignment.
Forms of Education	Formal, vocational, professional, lifelong learning.
NEP 2020 Role	Vocational training, multidisciplinary learning, technology integration.
Challenges	Quality gaps, skill mismatch, digital divide, limited vocational education, brain drain.
Strategies	Curriculum reform, vocational training, industry collaboration, technology use, teacher training, innovation.

Chapter 3

Agencies of Education

3.1 Formal Agencies of Education

Introduction

Education takes place in various ways and through different agencies. An **agency of education** is any institution, organisation, or arrangement that provides structured learning to individuals. These agencies can be broadly divided into:

1. **Formal**
2. **Non-formal**
3. **Informal**

In this section, we will focus on the **Formal Agency of Education**, which is the most organised and systematic form of learning.

Meaning of Formal Education

Formal education refers to the structured, organised form of learning that takes place in recognised institutions such as schools, colleges, universities, and training centres. It follows a fixed curriculum, a defined timetable, and a systematic evaluation process.

Simple definition: Formal education is planned education that happens in institutions following official rules and syllabi.

Features of Formal Education

Feature	Explanation
Systematic	Planned and organised with fixed objectives and syllabus.
Institutionalised	Takes place in recognised schools, colleges, and universities.
Structured Curriculum	Follows a predetermined course of study approved by authorities.
Timed	Operates according to a fixed timetable and academic calendar.
Certified	Provides recognised certificates or degrees.
Teacher-led	Guided and controlled by professional teachers.

Objectives of Formal Education

Formal education serves multiple purposes. Its key objectives include:

1. **Development of Knowledge:** Imparting theoretical and practical knowledge.
2. **Skill Acquisition:** Providing vocational and professional skills.
3. **Personality Development:** Shaping attitudes, values, and behaviours.
4. **Preparation for Higher Education and Employment:** Equipping students for further studies and job opportunities.

5. **Socialisation:** Preparing learners to become responsible citizens.
6. **Cultural Transmission:** Passing cultural values and heritage to the next generation.

Types of Formal Education

Formal education can be broadly classified into three levels:

Level of Education	Description
Primary Education	Basic education provided at elementary level (usually grades 1–5/6). Focuses on literacy, numeracy, and basic values.
Secondary Education	Middle and high school education (grades 6–12). Prepares students for higher education or vocational training.
Higher Education	University or college education leading to degrees and professional qualifications. Includes undergraduate, postgraduate, and research studies.

Characteristics of Formal Education

1. **Planned Learning:** Follows a structured syllabus prepared by educational authorities.
2. **Teacher-centred Learning:** Teachers are the primary source of knowledge.

3. **Assessment and Evaluation:** Regular exams, assignments, and evaluations to assess learning outcomes.
4. **Time-bound:** Has a fixed duration and defined stages of progression.
5. **Certification:** Students receive recognised certificates, diplomas, or degrees.
6. **Curriculum-based:** Learning is guided by official curriculum frameworks.

Role of Formal Education in Society

Formal education plays a crucial role in shaping individuals and society:

- **Knowledge Creation:** Formal education equips individuals with advanced knowledge and research skills.
- **Skill Development:** Prepares a skilled workforce essential for economic growth.
- **Socialisation:** Instils social norms, civic values, and ethical behaviour.
- **National Development:** Contributes to human resource development, scientific progress, and innovation.
- **Cultural Preservation:** Formal education transmits cultural heritage and values to new generations.

Examples of Formal Education Agencies

1. **Schools:** Primary, secondary, and senior secondary schools following state or national boards such as CBSE, ICSE, or State Boards.

2. **Colleges and Universities:** Provide undergraduate, postgraduate, and doctoral education.
3. **Professional Institutes:** For specialised education such as engineering, medicine, law, and management.
4. **Vocational Training Centres:** Offer training in trades, crafts, and technical fields.
5. **Distance Education Universities:** Such as Indira Gandhi National Open University (IGNOU), providing structured courses remotely.

Advantages of Formal Education

- Structured and planned learning environment.
- Recognised qualifications for employment and higher education.
- Access to qualified teachers and proper resources.
- Encourages discipline and systematic learning habits.
- Provides a clear career path and skill development.

Limitations of Formal Education

- Lack of flexibility in syllabus and methods.
- High cost of quality education.
- Focus on rote learning in some systems rather than critical thinking.
- Limited accessibility in rural and remote areas.
- May not fully address the individual needs and creativity of learners.

Formal Education in the Context of NEP 2020

The **National Education Policy 2020** emphasises making formal education more holistic, multidisciplinary, and skill-oriented. NEP aims to:

- Integrate vocational education from an early stage.
- Emphasise critical thinking, creativity, and experiential learning.
- Introduce flexibility in curriculum and assessment.
- Use technology for enhanced learning.
- Focus on multilingualism and value-based education.

This makes formal education under NEP 2020 a dynamic system aimed at developing human resources for a competitive global future.

3.2 Informal Agencies of Education

Introduction

Education does not only take place in schools or colleges. It is a lifelong process that happens everywhere — in homes, communities, workplaces, and social environments. These unstructured learning experiences occur through everyday life interactions.

Such learning is called **Informal Education**. It is one of the most natural and continuous forms of education and plays a vital role in shaping individuals' values, attitudes, behaviour, and personality.

Meaning of Informal Education

Informal education refers to the learning that takes place outside formal school settings without a fixed curriculum or timetable. It is unplanned, unstructured, and usually happens naturally as part of life experiences.

Simple definition: Informal education is the learning that happens through daily life, without formal teaching or organised classes.

Characteristics of Informal Education

Feature	Explanation
Unstructured	No fixed curriculum or timetable.
Lifelong	Happens throughout life, from childhood to old age.
Experiential	Learning through experience rather than formal instruction.
Social Interaction	Takes place through family, peers, work, and community interactions.
Voluntary	Learners engage willingly without compulsion.
Continuous	Happens throughout a person's life.

Sources of Informal Education

Informal education comes from various aspects of everyday life:

1. **Family:** Parents and relatives are the first educators of a child. Family teaches values, ethics, social behaviour, and cultural traditions.
2. **Peer Groups:** Friends and peers influence behaviour, attitudes, and skills through social interactions.
3. **Workplace:** On-the-job experiences develop technical skills, problem-solving abilities, and teamwork.
4. **Mass Media:** Television, radio, newspapers, internet, and social media provide information and shape opinions.
5. **Community and Cultural Activities:** Festivals, rituals, local traditions, and community work teach cultural values and social responsibilities.
6. **Self-learning:** Reading books, exploring the internet, and hobbies contribute to self-driven learning.

Objectives of Informal Education

Informal education aims to develop:

1. **Values and Ethics:** Instilling moral principles and civic responsibility.
2. **Social Skills:** Promoting communication, cooperation, and empathy.
3. **Cultural Awareness:** Preserving traditions, languages, and heritage.
4. **Personal Development:** Enhancing creativity, problem-solving, and adaptability.
5. **Lifelong Learning:** Encouraging curiosity and continuous self-improvement.

Features in Practice

Informal education is not confined to any institution. It happens naturally when an individual learns from:

- Observing others.
- Participating in social activities.
- Experiencing real-life situations.
- Interacting with elders and peers.
- Accessing information from media and technology.

Advantages of Informal Education

- Flexible and natural learning process.
- Develops social skills and moral values.
- Adaptable to individual needs and situations.
- Encourages creativity and problem-solving.
- Available to everyone without formal admission or fees.

Limitations of Informal Education

- Lacks systematic structure and formal certification.
- Quality of learning depends on personal and environmental factors.
- May not provide specialised knowledge needed for formal qualifications.
- Hard to measure and assess learning outcomes.
- Risk of misinformation from unreliable sources.

Informal Education in the Context of NEP 2020

The **National Education Policy 2020** recognises the importance of informal education as a complementary process to formal learning. NEP emphasises:

- Encouraging **self-learning** and curiosity-driven exploration.
- Promoting **community learning** through cultural and local knowledge.
- Using **digital platforms** and open resources to make informal education more accessible.
- Encouraging lifelong learning to adapt to a changing world.

NEP 2020 sees informal education as a vital component of a holistic education system that blends formal, non-formal, and informal methods to ensure a richer learning experience.

Examples of Informal Education

1. **Family Teaching:** Learning values, traditions, and language at home.
2. **Social Interaction:** Learning manners, cooperation, and problem-solving from friends.
3. **Media Learning:** Watching documentaries, listening to podcasts, and exploring online courses.
4. **Community Participation:** Volunteering in local projects and participating in cultural events.
5. **Self-directed Learning:** Reading books, online self-study, and learning hobbies like painting or coding.

Conclusion

Informal education is the most natural and ongoing form of learning. Unlike formal education, it does not follow a set syllabus, yet it plays a crucial role in personality development, cultural transmission, and lifelong learning. Under NEP 2020, informal education is recognised as a valuable complement to formal and non-formal education, creating a comprehensive ecosystem that fosters holistic development and prepares individuals for a dynamic future.

□ Summary Table — Informal Education

Aspect	Details
Meaning	Learning through daily life without structured classes or curriculum.
Characteristics	Unstructured, lifelong, experiential, voluntary, social.
Sources	Family, peers, workplace, mass media, community, self-learning.
Objectives	Values, social skills, cultural awareness, personal development.
Advantages	Flexible, accessible, develops life skills, cost-effective.
Limitations	Lack of structure, no certification, difficult to measure outcomes.
NEP 2020 Role	Promotes self-learning, community knowledge, digital learning, lifelong learning.

3.3 Non-Formal Agencies of Education

Introduction

Education occurs in many forms beyond the structured environment of schools and colleges. **Non-formal education** is a planned learning process that happens outside the formal school system. It is more flexible, learner-centred, and often designed for specific learning needs, especially for those who cannot access formal education or need additional skills.

Non-formal education plays a vital role in adult learning, skill development, and lifelong education. It bridges the gap between formal and informal education.

Meaning of Non-Formal Education

Non-formal education refers to organised learning activities that take place outside the formal school system. It is flexible in terms of time, curriculum, and methods. It caters to specific learning objectives, often focused on skill development, adult literacy, vocational training, and personal growth.

Simple definition: Non-formal education is planned education outside formal institutions, designed to meet particular learning needs and promote lifelong learning.

Characteristics of Non-Formal Education

Feature	Explanation
Flexible	No rigid timetable or syllabus; adaptable to learners' needs.
Learner-Centred	Focuses on the needs, interests, and abilities of learners.
Planned Learning	Organised and structured, though less rigid than formal education.
Accessibility	Designed to reach people of all ages, especially those outside formal schools.
Skill-Oriented	Emphasises practical skills and knowledge.
Voluntary	Participation is often optional, based on learners' interests.

Objectives of Non-Formal Education

The objectives of non-formal education include:

1. **Skill Development:** Providing practical skills for employment and livelihood.
2. **Adult Literacy:** Enhancing literacy and numeracy for those who missed formal schooling.
3. **Personal Development:** Encouraging critical thinking, self-reliance, and self-confidence.
4. **Community Development:** Helping communities grow through participatory learning.

5. **Lifelong Learning:** Offering flexible opportunities for continued learning.
6. **Social Awareness:** Promoting civic responsibility, health awareness, and cultural knowledge.

Types of Non-Formal Education

Non-formal education can take various forms:

Type	Description
Adult Education Programmes	Literacy and numeracy training for adults who missed formal schooling.
Vocational Training	Short-term skill training in trades like carpentry, tailoring, driving, etc.
Community Education	Learning programmes organised by community centres for cultural and social awareness.
Distance Learning	Learning via online or offline correspondence courses outside formal systems.
Continuing Education	Skill and knowledge enhancement courses for working professionals.
NGO-led Programmes	Non-governmental organisations providing education for health, literacy, and livelihood.

Role of Non-Formal Education

Non-formal education complements formal education by:

- Providing education for all, especially marginalised communities.
- Offering flexible learning opportunities for working individuals and adults.
- Enhancing employability through vocational and skill-based training.
- Promoting personal growth and social awareness.
- Encouraging community participation in education.

Advantages of Non-Formal Education

- Flexible structure tailored to learners' needs.
- Focuses on practical skills for real-life applications.
- Accessible to all age groups and communities.
- Encourages participation of disadvantaged groups.
- Supports lifelong learning and adaptability.

Limitations of Non-Formal Education

- Lack of formal recognition and certification in many cases.
- Limited resources compared to formal education.
- Irregular attendance and participation.
- Quality of teaching may vary.
- Less standardisation in curriculum and evaluation.

Non-Formal Education in the Context of NEP 2020

The **National Education Policy 2020** recognises the significance of non-formal education for achieving inclusive and equitable learning. NEP aims to:

- Integrate non-formal and vocational education within mainstream education.
- Provide flexible learning pathways for all age groups.
- Use digital tools and open learning resources to broaden access.
- Promote community-based learning and skill development.
- Encourage lifelong learning opportunities beyond formal institutions.

NEP 2020 envisions a learning ecosystem where non-formal education complements formal education and strengthens human resource development.

Examples of Non-Formal Education

1. **Adult Literacy Centres:** Government and NGO programmes teaching literacy to adults.
2. **Vocational Training Institutes:** Short-term courses for skill development.
3. **Online Learning Platforms:** Skill-based online courses offered through SWAYAM, Coursera, etc.
4. **Community Learning Centres:** Local programmes teaching life skills, health awareness, and cultural knowledge.
5. **Workplace Training:** On-the-job training for skill upgradation.

Conclusion

Non-formal education is an important part of the education ecosystem. It provides flexible, need-based learning opportunities for those who cannot participate in formal education. Under NEP 2020, non-formal education is recognised as a powerful means to achieve lifelong learning, skill development, and inclusive growth. It acts as a bridge between formal and informal education, enabling individuals to gain practical knowledge and skills for personal and social development.

□ Summary Table — Non-Formal Education

Aspect	Details
Meaning	Organised learning outside formal institutions to meet specific needs.
Characteristics	Flexible, learner-centred, accessible, skill-oriented, voluntary.
Objectives	Skill development, adult literacy, personal development, community development, lifelong learning.
Types	Adult education, vocational training, community education, distance learning, continuing education.
Advantages	Flexible, practical, accessible, inclusive.
Limitations	Lack of formal certification, fewer resources, irregular attendance, quality variation.

NEP 2020 Role	Integrating vocational training, flexible pathways, community learning, digital tools.

Chapter 4

Indian Constitution and Education

4.1 Inculcation of Constitutional Values in Education

Introduction

Education in a democratic society is not just about academic knowledge or vocational skills. It is also about developing responsible citizens who respect the principles of the Constitution. The **Indian Constitution** provides the foundation of democracy, justice, liberty, equality, fraternity, and fundamental rights.

Inculcation of **constitutional values** in education means integrating these principles into the teaching–learning process so that students not only understand them but also live by them in everyday life.

This is a core goal of the **National Education Policy (NEP) 2020**, which emphasises value-based education for fostering a socially responsible and cohesive society.

Meaning of Inculcation of Constitutional Values in Education

Inculcation means instilling values in a deep and lasting way. Constitutional values refer to the fundamental principles and ideals enshrined in the Constitution of India that guide governance, law, and civic life.

Thus, **inculcation of constitutional values in education** means teaching and integrating the constitutional principles into the entire educational process, so learners develop respect for the Constitution and practise democratic citizenship.

Simple definition: It is the process of embedding the values of the Constitution — such as justice, liberty, equality, fraternity, and dignity — into the knowledge, attitudes, and behaviours of students.

Core Constitutional Values in India

The Indian Constitution embodies several key values that need to be inculcated through education:

Constitutional Value	Meaning
Justice	Social, economic, and political justice ensuring fairness in society.
Liberty	Freedom of thought, expression, belief, faith, and worship.
Equality	Equal rights and opportunities for all without discrimination.
Fraternity	Promoting a sense of brotherhood and unity among citizens.
Secularism	Equal respect and treatment of all religions.

Democracy	Governance by the people, for the people, and of the people.
Fundamental Rights	Rights guaranteed to every citizen to live with dignity.

Importance of Inculcation of Constitutional Values in Education

1. **Strengthening Democracy:** Citizens aware of constitutional values participate meaningfully in democracy.
2. **Promoting Social Harmony:** Values like equality and fraternity reduce social discrimination and conflict.
3. **Ensuring Justice:** Education instils understanding of rights and responsibilities.
4. **Developing Responsible Citizenship:** Prepares students to actively contribute to the nation's welfare.
5. **Preserving Cultural Diversity:** Promotes respect for all religions, languages, and cultures.
6. **Preventing Corruption:** Ethical education reduces intolerance and misuse of power.

Objectives of Inculcation of Constitutional Values in Education

- To make students aware of their rights and duties as citizens.
- To develop a sense of patriotism and national unity.

- To promote equality, justice, and liberty in thought and action.
- To encourage respect for diversity, democracy, and secularism.
- To integrate constitutional values into daily life and decision-making.
- To create socially responsible and morally upright citizens.

The Role of Education in Inculcating Constitutional Values

Education is a powerful tool for nurturing constitutional values in the following ways:

1. **Knowledge Development:** Imparting knowledge about the Constitution and democratic principles.
2. **Attitude Formation:** Encouraging positive attitudes towards equality, justice, and liberty.
3. **Skill Development:** Developing skills for dialogue, conflict resolution, and democratic participation.
4. **Behavioural Change:** Translating knowledge and attitudes into responsible action.

Strategies for Inculcation of Constitutional Values in Education

To effectively inculcate constitutional values, education must go beyond textbooks and integrate values into teaching practices, school culture, and community activities.

1. Curriculum Integration

Constitutional values should be integrated into school and college syllabi, across subjects such as Political Science, History, Civics, and Ethics.

Examples:

- Teaching the Preamble of the Constitution in Social Science classes.
- Including case studies of landmark judgments in law courses.
- Discussing the importance of Fundamental Rights in Hindi or English classes.

2. Value-Based Teaching–Learning Methods

- **Discussion Method:** Encouraging debates and discussions on constitutional issues.
- **Project Method:** Assigning projects on civic responsibility, human rights, and constitutional history.
- **Role-Play:** Simulating democratic decision-making or legal processes to foster understanding.
- **Storytelling:** Using stories and biographies of freedom fighters and constitutional makers.

3. Experiential Learning

Learning constitutional values through real-life experiences:

- Organising visits to courts, legislative assemblies, and cultural centres.
- Community service projects such as cleanliness drives, voter awareness campaigns.
- Participating in social outreach programmes.

4. School and Campus Culture

- Promoting a democratic culture within schools through student councils, debates, and elections.
- Encouraging respect for diversity in language, culture, and religion.
- Observing Constitution Day (26 November) with programmes and activities.

5. Teacher's Role

Teachers must act as role models of constitutional values:

- Demonstrating fairness and respect in the classroom.
- Encouraging participation and critical thinking.
- Guiding students in applying values to real-life situations.

6. Use of Technology

Digital platforms can enhance awareness of constitutional values:

- E-learning modules on the Constitution.
- Online quizzes, discussion forums, and webinars on civic education.

- Interactive apps and resources for schools and colleges.

Role of NEP 2020 in Inculcating Constitutional Values

NEP 2020 highlights value-based education as central to the purpose of education. It calls for:

- Integrating constitutional values into the curriculum at all levels.
- Promoting **ethical and moral education** from foundational stages.
- Encouraging **critical thinking, dialogue, and participation** in democratic life.
- Using **multidisciplinary approaches** to teach values, linking them to science, arts, and humanities.
- Promoting **Indian knowledge systems** alongside constitutional education.

Challenges in Inculcation of Constitutional Values

1. **Lack of Awareness:** Students and teachers may lack adequate knowledge of the Constitution.
2. **Curriculum Overload:** Heavy syllabi leave little time for value education.
3. **Teacher Preparedness:** Teachers may not be adequately trained in value-based education.
4. **Cultural and Social Barriers:** Prejudices and discrimination hinder value education.
5. **Assessment Issues:** Difficulty in assessing internalisation of values.

6. **Impact of Media and Technology:** Negative influence of misinformation and polarising content.

Examples of Constitutional Values in Practice

- **Justice:** Judicial independence and landmark judgments protecting rights.
- **Liberty:** Freedom of expression in democratic discourse.
- **Equality:** Reservation policy and affirmative action for disadvantaged communities.
- **Fraternity:** Celebrating cultural festivals together.
- **Secularism:** Equal respect for all religions in educational institutions.

Model for Inculcation of Constitutional Values

A practical model could involve:

1. **Knowledge:** Teaching constitutional history, Preamble, Fundamental Rights and Duties.
2. **Understanding:** Classroom discussions, debates, and projects to deepen comprehension.
3. **Attitude:** Encouraging empathy, tolerance, and responsibility.
4. **Practice:** Student participation in democratic processes and social action projects.

Impact of Inculcating Constitutional Values

- Promotes **social cohesion** and national integration.

- Reduces discrimination and inequality.
- Strengthens democracy and rule of law.
- Prepares responsible citizens who can uphold the Constitution.
- Builds moral and ethical strength in society.

Conclusion

Inculcation of constitutional values in education is not optional; it is a necessity for a vibrant democracy like India. Education must not only impart knowledge but also mould the character of citizens who live by the ideals of justice, liberty, equality, and fraternity.

NEP 2020 provides a strong framework to integrate constitutional values into education through curriculum reforms, teacher training, value-based teaching, and experiential learning.

Ultimately, the goal is to make every learner a conscious citizen who understands and practices the spirit of the Constitution, thereby contributing to nation-building and sustaining democratic ideals.

□ Summary Table — Inculcation of Constitutional Values in Education

Aspect	Details
Meaning	Instilling constitutional values into education for responsible citizenship.
Core Values	Justice, liberty, equality, fraternity, secularism, democracy.

Importance	Strengthens democracy, promotes harmony, ensures justice, develops responsibility.
Objectives	Awareness of rights and duties, respect for diversity, fostering patriotism, promoting equality.
Strategies	Curriculum integration, value-based teaching, experiential learning, school culture, teacher role, technology use.
Challenges	Lack of awareness, curriculum overload, teacher preparedness, social barriers, assessment issues.
NEP 2020 Role	Integrates values into curriculum, promotes ethics, encourages participation, uses multidisciplinary approach.

4.2 Constitutional Provisions for Education

Introduction

Education is a fundamental pillar of nation-building. In India, the right to education is guaranteed by the Constitution. The framers of the Indian Constitution recognised education as essential for individual development and national progress.

Several provisions in the Constitution ensure access to education for all citizens, promote equality in education, and establish education as a concurrent subject for governance.

Understanding these constitutional provisions is crucial for students, teachers, and policy-makers to ensure effective implementation of educational policies such as the **National Education Policy (NEP) 2020**.

Meaning of Constitutional Provisions for Education

Constitutional provisions for education refer to the specific articles, schedules, and amendments in the Constitution of India that define the right to education, responsibilities of the state and citizens, and the framework for delivering education.

These provisions ensure that education in India is:

- Universal
- Accessible
- Equitable
- Relevant

Importance of Constitutional Provisions for Education

- Provides a **legal framework** for education in India.
- Guarantees the **Right to Education** to all citizens.
- Ensures **equal opportunities** in education without discrimination.
- Defines the responsibilities of the **Union and State Governments**.
- Guides policy-making in education.

Key Constitutional Provisions for Education in India

1. Article 21A — Right to Education

- Inserted by the **86th Constitutional Amendment Act, 2002**.

- States: *"The State shall provide free and compulsory education to all children of the age of six to fourteen years in such manner as the State may, by law, determine."*
- This provision makes education a **fundamental right** for children between 6 and 14 years of age.

Significance:

- Guarantees free and compulsory elementary education.
- Forms the legal basis for the **Right of Children to Free and Compulsory Education Act, 2009 (RTE Act)**.
- Establishes the state's responsibility for providing education.

2. Article 45 — Early Childhood Education

- Originally part of the Directive Principles of State Policy (DPSP).
- States: *"The State shall endeavour to provide early childhood care and education for all children until they complete the age of six years."*
- NEP 2020 emphasises the importance of early childhood care and education (ECCE) as foundational for lifelong learning.

Significance:

- Recognises early education as essential for holistic development.
- Guides policies for pre-primary education and early learning centres.

3. Article 29 and Article 30 — Protection of Minority Rights in Education

- **Article 29:** Protects the interests of minorities by allowing them to preserve their language, script, and culture.
- **Article 30:** Gives minorities the right to establish and administer educational institutions of their choice.

Significance:

- Promotes cultural diversity and protection of minority educational rights.
- Encourages participation of minorities in educational development.

4. Article 41 and Article 45 — Directive Principles of State Policy

- **Article 41:** The State shall, within its means, provide education and public assistance in cases of unemployment, old age, sickness, and disablement.
- **Article 45:** Promotes free and compulsory education for children, as already mentioned.

Significance:

- DPSPs guide the state in framing educational policies.
- Ensure that education is a state priority for social welfare.

5. Seventh Schedule — Distribution of Educational Responsibilities

- Education is a **concurrent subject** under the **Seventh Schedule of the Constitution**, meaning both Union and State Governments can legislate on it.
- **Entry 11 of List III (Concurrent List):** Relates to education.

Significance:

- Promotes cooperation between Union and States for educational planning.
- Allows flexibility in implementing education policies according to local needs.

6. Article 51A — Fundamental Duties

- Added by the **42nd Constitutional Amendment Act, 1976**.
- Article 51A(k) states: *"It shall be the duty of every citizen of India who is a parent or guardian to provide opportunities for education to his child or ward between the age of six and fourteen years."*

Significance:

- Reinforces the citizen's responsibility in education.
- Complements the Right to Education under Article 21A.

7. 86th Constitutional Amendment Act, 2002

- Made education a **fundamental right** by inserting Article 21A.
- Strengthened the state's commitment to universalising elementary education.

Significance:

- Provides a constitutional guarantee for free and compulsory education.
- Strengthens accountability of the state and local bodies in education.

Implications of Constitutional Provisions for Education

The constitutional provisions for education have led to:

- **Formulation of the RTE Act, 2009:** Gives practical effect to Article 21A.
- **Development of educational policies:** Such as NEP 2020, which aligns with constitutional values.
- **Access and Equity:** Emphasis on inclusive education for all, including marginalised groups.
- **Cultural Preservation:** Through protection of minority educational rights.
- **Accountability:** State governments and the Union Government are constitutionally bound to provide education.

Challenges in Implementing Constitutional Provisions

- Poor infrastructure and inadequate teacher training.
- Low enrolment and high dropout rates in rural areas.
- Social inequality and economic barriers to education.
- Inadequate budgetary allocation for education.
- Lack of awareness among citizens about their educational rights.

Role of NEP 2020 in Upholding Constitutional Provisions

NEP 2020 aligns with the constitutional vision for education:

- Strengthens **free and compulsory education** for ages 6–18.
- Promotes **equity and inclusion** for marginalised groups.
- Ensures **multilingual education** in early years, respecting cultural diversity.
- Encourages **vocational training** and skill development.
- Emphasises the holistic development of students, not just academic achievement.

Case Study: Right to Education in Practice

The **Right of Children to Free and Compulsory Education Act, 2009** is the most important legislative step taken to fulfil constitutional provisions.

Key features:

- Free education to children aged 6–14 years.

- Prohibition of detention for students up to class VIII.
- Reservation of seats for disadvantaged groups.
- Emphasis on child-centred and activity-based learning.

This Act reflects the spirit of constitutional provisions and makes them practical and enforceable.

Conclusion

The constitutional provisions for education in India form the legal backbone of the country's education system. They guarantee education as a fundamental right, protect the rights of minorities, ensure equality and inclusivity, and promote early childhood care and education.

NEP 2020 builds on these constitutional principles by envisioning a holistic, inclusive, and multidisciplinary education system that aligns with democratic values and prepares citizens for a dynamic future.

Constitutional provisions are not just legal requirements; they are the moral and democratic commitments of the nation to ensure that every child has the opportunity to learn, grow, and contribute to society.

□ Summary Table — Constitutional Provisions for Education

Provision	Description	Significance
Article 21A	Right to free and compulsory education	Legal guarantee for elementary education.

	for ages 6–14.	
Article 45	Early childhood care and education.	Foundation for holistic development.
Articles 29 & 30	Protection of minority educational rights.	Promotes cultural diversity and minority education.
Article 41	Right to public assistance and education.	Guides welfare-based educational policy.
Article 51A(k)	Duty of citizens to provide education to children.	Encourages societal responsibility.
Seventh Schedule	Education as a concurrent subject.	Cooperation between Union and States.
86th Constitutional Amendment	Made education a fundamental right.	Strengthens the legal basis for education.

Practice Questions

1. Objective Questions (MCQs)

1. Which Article of the Indian Constitution guarantees the right to free and compulsory education for children aged 6–14 years?
   a) Article 45
   b) Article 21A
   c) Article 29

d) Article 41

Answer: b) Article 21A

2. The Directive Principle related to early childhood education is given in:

   a) Article 45

   b) Article 41

   c) Article 29

   d) Article 51A

   Answer: a) Article 45

3. Which Article gives minorities the right to establish and administer educational institutions?

   a) Article 30

   b) Article 29

   c) Article 51A

   d) Article 21A

   Answer: a) Article 30

4. Fundamental Duties related to education are mentioned in:

   a) Article 41

   b) Article 45

   c) Article 51A(k)

   d) Article 21A

   Answer: c) Article 51A(k)

5. Education is listed as a __________ subject in the Seventh Schedule of the Indian Constitution.

   a) Union

   b) State

   c) Concurrent

   d) Residuary

   Answer: c) Concurrent

6. Which Constitutional Amendment made education a fundamental right in India?
   a) 42nd Amendment
   b) 44th Amendment
   c) 86th Amendment
   d) 73rd Amendment
   Answer: c) 86th Amendment
7. The Preamble of the Constitution reflects which constitutional value?
   a) Justice
   b) Liberty
   c) Equality
   d) All of the above
   Answer: d) All of the above

2. Short Answer Questions

1. Define inculcation of constitutional values in education.
2. Mention any four core constitutional values enshrined in the Indian Constitution.
3. What is the significance of Article 21A in the Indian Constitution?
4. Explain the role of Article 45 in early childhood education.
5. What is the role of education in strengthening democracy?
6. Mention any three objectives of inculcating constitutional values in education.
7. State the significance of Article 29 and Article 30.
8. What is the role of NEP 2020 in inculcating constitutional values?

9. Explain the importance of constitutional provisions for education.
10. What is the significance of making education a concurrent subject in the Constitution?

3. Long Answer Questions

1. Explain the meaning and importance of inculcation of constitutional values in education.
2. Describe the core constitutional values that should be inculcated through education.
3. Discuss the strategies for inculcating constitutional values in education with examples.
4. Analyse the constitutional provisions for education in India.
5. Explain the role of Article 21A and the Right to Education Act, 2009 in ensuring free and compulsory education in India.
6. Examine the role of NEP 2020 in integrating constitutional values into education.
7. Discuss the challenges in inculcating constitutional values in education.
8. Explain the significance of Articles 29 and 30 in protecting minority educational rights.
9. Discuss how constitutional provisions ensure equality and inclusivity in education.
10. Evaluate the role of education in promoting justice, liberty, equality, and fraternity as envisaged in the Constitution.

Chapter 5

Pre-Primary Education

5.1 Concept, Aims and Importance

Introduction

Education begins from the earliest stages of life. The early years are crucial for the physical, cognitive, emotional, and social development of children. This stage is known as **Pre-Primary Education**. It caters to children before they enter formal schooling, usually between the ages of 3 to 6 years.

In India, the **National Education Policy (NEP) 2020** recognises this stage as the foundation of education because pre-primary education forms the first step in a child's lifelong learning journey.

1. Concept of Pre-Primary Education

Pre-Primary Education refers to the initial stage of formal learning for children aged between 3 and 6 years. At this stage, learning occurs primarily through play, activities, and social experiences rather than structured classroom teaching.

It is the preparatory stage before formal schooling where children develop communication skills, basic knowledge, and social understanding through activities like storytelling, games, art, and group work.

In simple words: Pre-primary education is an early stage of learning where children develop foundational skills, attitudes, and knowledge that prepare them for formal schooling.

2. Aims of Pre-Primary Education

The main aims of pre-primary education are as follows:

Aim	Description
Child Development	To ensure the physical, mental, emotional, and social development of children.
Learning Through Play and Activities	To encourage children to learn through play and activity-based experiences, fostering creativity and critical thinking.
Language Development	To develop communication and language skills in children.
Social Skills	To foster social behaviour, cooperation, coexistence, and moral values.
Interest in Learning	To cultivate curiosity and enthusiasm for learning.
Independence and Self-reliance	To help children develop decision-making skills and self-confidence.

3. Importance of Pre-Primary Education

Pre-primary education is a foundation for lifelong learning and development. Its key importance includes:

3.1 Foundation for Child Development

- Lays the groundwork for cognitive, social, emotional, and physical development.
- Early learning experiences shape the ability to learn throughout life.

3.2 Social and Emotional Development

- Promotes cooperation, empathy, and moral values through group activities.
- Builds self-confidence and a positive self-image.

3.3 Developing Interest and Habits for Learning

- Learning through games, storytelling, art, and activities makes education enjoyable, fostering curiosity.
- Establishes the habit of learning, which continues throughout life.

3.4 Preparation for Formal Schooling

- Prepares children for the structure, discipline, and learning style of formal education.
- Helps children develop attention span and the habit of following rules.

3.5 Foundation for Inclusive Education

- Provides equal opportunities for all children, regardless of social, economic, or linguistic background.
- Encourages respect for diversity and coexistence.

4. NEP 2020 Perspective on Pre-Primary Education

NEP 2020 emphasises the importance of the **Foundational Stage of Education**. Key points include:

- Priority for **play-based and activity-based learning** for children aged 3–6 years.
- ECCE (Early Childhood Care and Education) should integrate all aspects of child development.
- Education should be **multilingual and culturally inclusive**.
- Pre-primary education should focus on games, art, culture, and language development.

NEP 2020 aims to make pre-primary education **accessible, equitable, and high quality for all children**, ensuring a strong foundation for lifelong learning.

5. Summary Table

Aspect	Details
Meaning	The first stage of education for children aged 3–6 years, focusing on play-based and activity-based learning.

Aims	Child development, language development, social skills, interest in learning, independence.
Importance	Foundation for child development, social and emotional growth, learning interest, preparation for formal education, inclusive education.
NEP 2020 Perspective	Foundational stage learning with play-based activities, ECCE, multilingual and culturally inclusive approaches.

5.2 Models of Pre-Primary Education

Pre-primary education can be delivered through different models, each with its own philosophy, structure, and teaching methods. Among the most influential models are the **Dalton Plan, Montessori Method, and Kindergarten Model**. These approaches guide educators in creating a nurturing and effective early learning environment.

1. Dalton Plan

The Dalton Plan was developed by Helen Parkhurst in the early 20th century. It is an educational model designed to give children independence, responsibility, and a sense of self-direction in learning.

Key Features:

- **Freedom and Responsibility:** Children have the freedom to choose their work but are responsible for completing tasks.
- **Individualised Learning:** Students work at their own pace, promoting self-learning and self-discipline.
- **Learning Contracts:** Children have assignments or "contracts" to be completed within a specific timeframe.
- **Teacher as Guide:** Teachers act as facilitators rather than direct instructors.

Application in Pre-Primary Education:

- Encourages curiosity and self-directed learning in early childhood.
- Promotes decision-making skills and independence.
- Fosters intrinsic motivation rather than extrinsic reward.

Advantages:

- Develops autonomy and responsibility.
- Encourages personalised learning.
- Builds organisational skills in children.

Limitations:

- Requires a highly prepared environment and trained teachers.
- May be challenging for very young children who need structured guidance.

2. Montessori Method

The Montessori Method was developed by Dr. Maria Montessori in the early 1900s. It is one of the most widely adopted models of pre-primary education in the world.

Key Principles:

- **Child-Centered Learning:** Education is tailored to each child's interests and developmental pace.
- **Prepared Environment:** Classrooms are equipped with specific learning materials designed for self-directed learning.
- **Sensory-Based Learning:** Activities are designed to develop the five senses through hands-on experiences.
- **Mixed Age Groups:** Children of different ages learn together to encourage peer learning.
- **Freedom Within Limits:** Children can choose activities but within a prepared and guided structure.

Application in Pre-Primary Education:

- Classrooms are designed as stimulating environments with learning corners for various activities.
- Focus on practical life skills, language development, mathematics, sensory education, and cultural studies.

Advantages:

- Encourages independence and self-discipline.

- Develops cognitive, social, and motor skills.
- Respects individual learning pace and interests.

Limitations:

- Requires specialised training for teachers.
- Needs investment in Montessori materials and environment.
- Less emphasis on group learning and structured lessons.

3. Kindergarten Model

The Kindergarten model was introduced by Friedrich Froebel in the early 19th century and is considered the foundation of modern early childhood education.

Key Principles:

- **Learning Through Play:** Play is the central activity for learning.
- **Holistic Development:** Focus on physical, social, emotional, and intellectual growth.
- **Use of Gifts and Occupations:** Froebel developed "gifts" (educational toys) and "occupations" (creative activities) to stimulate learning.
- **Integration of Nature:** Activities involve nature, art, and music to enhance learning.
- **Teacher's Role:** Teachers act as guides and facilitators.

Application in Pre-Primary Education:

- Curriculum focuses on activities such as storytelling, drawing, singing, dancing, and outdoor play.
- Learning is experiential and joyful.
- Emphasis on social interaction and creativity.

Advantages:

- Promotes creativity and imagination.
- Encourages cooperative learning and social skills.
- Integrates learning with natural experiences.

Limitations:

- Less structured approach may affect readiness for formal schooling.
- Requires well-trained teachers and resources for play-based learning.

Summary Table: Models of Pre-Primary Education

Model	Key Features	Advantages	Limitations
Dalton Plan	Freedom, responsibility, individualised learning, contracts	Develops autonomy, personalised learning, organisational skills	Needs prepared environment, difficult for very young children

Montessori	Child-centred, prepared environment, sensory learning, mixed age groups, freedom within limits	Promotes independence, respects pace, develops multiple skills	Needs specialised training, costly materials, less group learning
Kindergarten	Learning through play, holistic development, gifts and occupations, integration of nature	Encourages creativity, cooperative learning, social skills	Less structured, needs trained teachers and resources

Conclusion

The Dalton, Montessori, and Kindergarten models offer unique approaches to pre-primary education. While Dalton focuses on self-directed learning and responsibility, Montessori emphasises independence, sensory exploration, and a prepared learning environment. The Kindergarten model integrates play, creativity, and holistic development as the core of early education.

Each model has its strengths and limitations, and in modern pre-primary education—especially in the context of **NEP 2020**—a blended approach is often used to meet the needs of diverse learners and prepare them for lifelong learning.

5.3 Present Status of Pre-Primary Education in India

1. Enrollment Trends and Statistics

- **Enrollment Numbers**: As of the 2022–23 academic year, approximately **1 crore children** were enrolled in pre-primary education in India, a slight decline from **1.1 crore** in the previous year.
- **Gross Enrollment Ratio (GER)**: India's GER for pre-primary education stands at **51.69%** as of 2021, a decrease from **61.09%** in 2020. This is slightly below the global average of **52.40%**.
- **Age-wise Enrollment**: Among five-year-olds, **60.3%** were enrolled in primary education in 2023, indicating an early transition to formal schooling.

2. Infrastructure and Access

- **Urban-Rural Disparity**: Access to quality pre-primary education is significantly higher in urban areas compared to rural regions. Urban centers like Delhi, Mumbai, and Bengaluru have a higher concentration of quality preschools, whereas rural areas face challenges in infrastructure and availability.
- **Government Initiatives**: The government has introduced programs such as the **Annie Braille device** in Prayagraj to assist visually impaired students, showcasing efforts to make learning more inclusive.

3. Quality of Education

- **Curriculum and Pedagogy**: Despite the emphasis on Early Childhood Care and Education (ECCE) in NEP 2020, many Anganwadi Centres and government-funded preschools struggle to provide holistic educational experiences due to inadequate resources and infrastructure.
- **Teacher Training**: There is a substantial shortage of trained and dedicated teachers in the pre-primary sector. According to the National Family Health Survey (NFHS-5), only **13.6%** of children aged 5 years attended pre-primary schooling, highlighting the need for improved teacher training and professional development.

4. Socioeconomic and Regional Inequalities

- **Access Disparities**: Children from lower castes, rural areas, and economically disadvantaged backgrounds have limited access to quality pre-primary education. Estimates from the National Sample Survey (NSS) indicate that only around **20%** of children aged 3–5 years are attending pre-primary education in India, with significant variations across different states.
- **Gender and Community Gaps**: Muslim children and those from marginalized communities face additional barriers to accessing early childhood education, exacerbating existing educational inequalities.

5. Policy and Future Outlook

- **NEP 2020 Goals**: The National Education Policy 2020 aims to achieve universal provisioning and quality early childhood education by 2030. This includes integrating pre-primary education into the formal education system and enhancing the quality of ECCE programs.
- **Investment in Infrastructure**: The Indian preschool market is projected to reach **$10.2 billion by 2032**, indicating a growing recognition of the importance of early childhood education and potential for increased investment.

Summary Table: Current Status of Pre-Primary Education in India

Aspect	Current Status
Enrollment Rate	Approximately 1 crore children enrolled; GER at 51.69% (2021)
Urban-Rural Access	Higher access in urban areas; significant disparities in rural regions
Infrastructure Quality	Inadequate in many government-funded centers; need for improvement
Teacher Training	Shortage of trained educators; only 13.6% of 5-year-olds attend pre-primary
Socioeconomic Disparities	Limited access for marginalized communities; regional variations

Policy Initiatives	NEP 2020 aims for universal and quality ECCE by 2030; increased market investment

5.4 National Education Policy (NEP) 2020 and Pre-Primary Education

Introduction

The National Education Policy (NEP) 2020 represents a significant shift in India's educational framework, emphasizing the importance of early childhood education. Recognizing the critical developmental phase between ages 3 and 8, the policy introduces a restructured 5+3+3+4 curricular framework, where the first five years constitute the **Foundational Stage**. This stage encompasses three years of pre-primary education (ages 3–6) and two years of early primary schooling (Grades 1 and 2, ages 6–8).

Key Provisions of NEP 2020 for Pre-Primary Education

1. Universal Access and Quality

- **Universalization of Early Childhood Care and Education (ECCE):** The policy aims to ensure that every child has access to quality pre-primary education, integrating Anganwadi centers and preschools into the formal education system.
- **Infrastructure Development:** Emphasis is placed on creating child-friendly learning environments with

appropriate infrastructure, including safe play areas and learning materials.

2. Play-Based and Activity-Based Learning

- **Curriculum Framework:** The NEP advocates for a curriculum that is flexible, play-based, and activity-based, focusing on holistic development rather than rote learning.
- **Pedagogical Approaches:** Teaching methods are designed to be engaging and enjoyable, fostering creativity, critical thinking, and problem-solving skills in young learners.

3. Teacher Training and Professional Development

- **Specialized Training:** The policy calls for the establishment of a dedicated cadre of teachers for the foundational stage, with specialized training in early childhood education.
- **Continuous Professional Development:** Ongoing training programs are to be implemented to enhance teachers' skills and knowledge, ensuring high-quality education delivery.

4. Integration with Formal Education

- **Smooth Transition:** Efforts are made to ensure a seamless transition from pre-primary education to formal schooling, with continuity in curriculum and pedagogy.
- **Curricular Alignment:** The foundational stage curriculum is aligned with the National Curriculum Framework (NCF) to maintain consistency and coherence in educational content.

Implementation Strategies

- **Community Engagement:** Active involvement of communities and parents is encouraged to support children's learning and development.
- **Monitoring and Evaluation:** Mechanisms for regular assessment and feedback are established to monitor the effectiveness of pre-primary education programs and make necessary adjustments.
- **Policy Support:** State governments are urged to formulate policies that support the objectives of the NEP, including regulatory frameworks for private preschools and integration of pre-primary education into the formal education system.

Challenges and Opportunities

Challenges

- **Resource Constraints:** Limited financial and infrastructural resources may hinder the effective implementation of the policy's provisions.
- **Teacher Shortage:** The lack of adequately trained teachers poses a significant challenge to delivering quality pre-primary education.
- **Regional Disparities:** Variations in the availability and quality of pre-primary education across different regions can lead to inequities.

Opportunities

- **Policy Support:** The NEP provides a comprehensive framework for improving early childhood education, offering opportunities for systemic reforms.
- **Community Involvement:** Engaging communities in the educational process can enhance the relevance and effectiveness of pre-primary education programs.
- **Technological Integration:** Leveraging technology can support innovative teaching methods and expand access to quality educational resources.

Practice Questions

A. Short Answer Questions

1. What is the importance of the Foundational Stage in NEP 2020?
2. What are the main changes proposed in NEP 2020 for pre-primary education?
3. Explain the significance of play-based learning according to NEP 2020.
4. What is the purpose of Early Childhood Care and Education (ECCE) in NEP 2020?
5. What provisions does NEP 2020 make for teacher training in pre-primary education?

B. Long Answer Questions

1. Analyse the key provisions for pre-primary education proposed in the National Education Policy 2020.
2. Explain the importance of play-based and activity-based learning in pre-primary education according to NEP 2020.
3. Discuss the features and objectives of the Foundational Stage under NEP 2020 in detail.
4. Discuss the role of teacher training and professional development in pre-primary education as proposed in NEP 2020.
5. Present your views on the current status of pre-primary education in India from the perspective of NEP 2020.

C. Multiple Choice Questions (MCQs)

1. What is the duration of the Foundational Stage in NEP 2020?
   a) 3 years
   b) 5 years
   c) 7 years
   d) 4 years
2. According to NEP 2020, what is the main objective of pre-primary education?
   a) Only language development
   b) Holistic development
   c) Only mathematical skills
   d) Only learning habit
3. What is the full form of ECCE in NEP 2020?
   a) Early Child Care and Education
   b) Early Childhood Care and Education

c) Early Child Curriculum Education
d) Early Child Cognitive Education

4. NEP 2020 proposes integrating pre-primary education with which stage of education?
a) Higher education
b) Primary education
c) Secondary education
d) Adult education

Chapter 6

Primary and Secondary Education

6.1 Concept, Aims, and Importance of Secondary Education

Introduction

Secondary education serves as a pivotal stage in an individual's educational journey, bridging the foundational learning acquired in primary education with the specialized knowledge imparted in higher education. It encompasses the middle and high school years, typically from grades 6 to 12, and plays a crucial role in shaping the intellectual, social, and emotional development of adolescents.

Concept of Secondary Education

Secondary education is designed to provide students with a broad general education, preparing them for further academic pursuits, vocational training, or entry into the workforce. It builds upon the foundational skills acquired in primary education, such as literacy and numeracy, and introduces students to a wider range of subjects, including sciences, humanities, and arts.

In many educational systems, secondary education is divided into two stages:

- **Lower Secondary Education**: Often referred to as middle school or junior high, this stage typically includes grades 6 to 8. It focuses on reinforcing basic skills and introducing students to a broader curriculum.
- **Upper Secondary Education**: Corresponding to high school, this stage includes grades 9 to 12 and offers more specialized subjects, allowing students to explore areas of interest in greater depth.

Aims of Secondary Education

The objectives of secondary education are multifaceted, aiming to:

1. **Provide a Broad Knowledge Base**: Equip students with a comprehensive understanding of various subjects, fostering intellectual curiosity and critical thinking.
2. **Develop Practical Skills**: Impart skills that are applicable in real-world scenarios, such as problem-solving, communication, and teamwork.
3. **Prepare for Higher Education**: Lay the groundwork for advanced studies by offering subjects that align with tertiary education requirements.
4. **Facilitate Career Readiness**: Introduce vocational training and career guidance to help students make informed decisions about their future professions.
5. **Promote Social and Emotional Development**: Support the growth of students' social skills, emotional intelligence, and ethical values.
6. **Encourage Civic Responsibility**: Instill a sense of civic duty and awareness of societal issues, preparing students to be active and responsible citizens.

Importance of Secondary Education

Secondary education holds significant importance for individuals and society at large:

1. Academic Development

Secondary education deepens students' knowledge in various subjects, enhancing their intellectual capabilities. It encourages analytical thinking, creativity, and the ability to synthesize information, which are essential skills in the modern world.

2. Career Opportunities

A secondary education diploma is often a prerequisite for many jobs and serves as a stepping stone to higher education. It opens doors to a wide range of career paths, from technical professions to academic fields.

3. Personal Growth

The adolescent years are critical for personal development. Secondary education provides an environment where students can explore their interests, develop self-confidence, and build resilience.

4. Social Integration

Schools serve as microcosms of society, where students learn to interact with peers from diverse backgrounds. This fosters social cohesion, empathy, and respect for diversity.

5. Economic Impact

Educated individuals are more likely to contribute positively to the economy. Secondary education enhances employability, leading to higher income levels and economic stability.

6. Societal Progress

A well-educated populace is essential for the advancement of society. Secondary education promotes informed decision-making, active participation in democratic processes, and the development of a knowledgeable citizenry.

Global Perspectives on Secondary Education

Different countries have unique approaches to secondary education, influenced by cultural, economic, and historical factors. For instance, in Finland, the emphasis is on equality and student well-being, with less standardized testing and a focus on individualized learning. In contrast, countries like Japan prioritize discipline and academic excellence, with rigorous entrance exams determining access to higher education institutions.

International organizations, such as UNESCO, advocate for inclusive and equitable secondary education, emphasizing the need for quality education that caters to all students, regardless of their socio-economic background.

Challenges in Secondary Education

Despite its importance, secondary education faces several challenges:

- **Access and Equity**: In many parts of the world, especially in developing countries, access to quality secondary education is limited due to factors like poverty, gender discrimination, and geographical barriers.
- **Quality of Education**: Variations in the quality of education can result from inadequate infrastructure, lack of trained teachers, and outdated curricula.

- **Dropout Rates**: High dropout rates, particularly among marginalized groups, hinder the achievement of universal secondary education.
- **Relevance to Job Market**: There is often a disconnect between the skills taught in schools and those demanded by employers, leading to underemployment among graduates.

Initiatives to Improve Secondary Education

To address these challenges, various initiatives have been implemented:

- **Policy Reforms**: Governments are revising educational policies to promote inclusivity, quality, and relevance in secondary education.
- **International Programs**: Organizations like UNESCO and UNICEF support global efforts to improve secondary education through funding, research, and advocacy.
- **Community Engagement**: Involving communities in the educational process ensures that the needs and aspirations of students are met.
- **Curriculum Development**: Updating curricula to include life skills, vocational training, and digital literacy prepares students for the modern workforce.

6.2 Present Status of Primary Education in India

Introduction

Primary education in India is a fundamental right under Article 21-A of the Constitution, ensuring free and compulsory education for children aged 6 to 14 years. Over the years, India has made substantial progress in expanding access to primary education. However, quality, infrastructure, and equity issues remain challenges. This essay examines the current status of primary education in India, exploring achievements, challenges, and reforms.

Enrollment and Access

India's school education system currently serves millions of students across a large number of schools, with government schools constituting the majority. Gross Enrollment Ratio (GER) at the primary level is high, approaching universal enrollment. Significant progress has been made in enrollment rates across rural and urban areas, although disparities exist in certain regions.

Despite near-universal enrollment at the primary stage, challenges like out-of-school children, particularly among marginalized communities, still persist. Efforts by the government, non-government organizations, and international bodies have been instrumental in improving access to primary education.

Quality of Education

Enrollment does not necessarily ensure quality education. Reports indicate that a considerable proportion of students in rural India struggle with basic reading and arithmetic skills. This is a critical concern because foundational learning forms the basis for higher education and life-long learning.

Factors affecting quality include inadequate teacher training, outdated teaching methodologies, lack of learning materials, and limited use of technology in classrooms. In addition, large class sizes and high student-teacher ratios further reduce the quality of education delivery.

Infrastructure and Resources

Infrastructure is a key determinant of education quality. Significant progress has been made in improving school infrastructure in India. Many schools now have access to electricity, drinking water, separate toilets for boys and girls, playgrounds, and libraries. Moreover, initiatives have increased the presence of computers and internet facilities in schools.

Nevertheless, disparities in infrastructure remain, especially in rural and remote areas where schools often lack basic facilities. This impacts the learning environment and student engagement, particularly for disadvantaged children.

Teacher Training and Professional Development

Teachers are central to the quality of primary education. National policies emphasize the need for continuous professional development for teachers. Initiatives like specialized training programs aim to improve teachers' pedagogical skills, subject knowledge, and use of technology in teaching.

However, the quality and coverage of teacher training programs vary across states. Many teachers face challenges such as inadequate training, lack of resources, and limited professional support, affecting their ability to deliver effective teaching.

Inclusive Education

Inclusive education is vital to ensure that children from all backgrounds, including those with disabilities or from marginalized communities, have equal access to quality education. India has made significant progress in implementing inclusive education under schemes like the Samagra Shiksha Abhiyan.

Special initiatives, such as providing assistive devices, inclusive classrooms, and support for children with special needs, have been introduced in some states. While these initiatives are commendable, inclusive education still needs wider implementation to reach all children in need.

Policy Initiatives and Reforms

Several policy frameworks have shaped primary education in India:

- **The Right to Education (RTE) Act, 2009**: Guarantees free and compulsory education for children aged 6–14 years and mandates norms for infrastructure, teacher qualifications, and student-teacher ratios.
- **The National Education Policy (NEP) 2020**: Advocates universal foundational literacy and numeracy by Grade 3 and promotes a 5+3+3+4 curricular structure that integrates early

childhood care and education with primary schooling. It emphasizes activity-based and experiential learning, multilingual education, and teacher capacity building.

- **Samagra Shiksha Abhiyan**: Aims at holistic development of school education from pre-primary to senior secondary levels by improving quality, access, equity, and infrastructure.

These reforms and policies are designed to address the gaps in access, quality, and inclusivity in primary education.

Challenges

Despite significant progress, challenges persist:

- **Quality of Learning**: Low learning outcomes continue to be a challenge. Many children reach higher grades without mastering foundational literacy and numeracy skills.
- **Infrastructure Gaps**: Rural and remote schools often lack basic facilities such as clean drinking water, electricity, functional toilets, and proper classrooms.
- **Teacher Shortages**: Shortages of trained teachers, particularly in rural areas, result in poor learning environments.
- **Dropout Rates**: While dropout rates at the primary level have declined significantly, issues of retention remain, especially in disadvantaged communities.
- **Equity and Inclusion**: Socio-economic, gender, and regional disparities still affect access to quality education.

Recent Initiatives and Innovations

Recent years have seen various initiatives to improve primary education:

- Integration of technology in classrooms to enhance teaching and learning experiences.
- Community participation programs to strengthen school governance and accountability.
- Curriculum reforms to make learning more engaging and relevant.
- Special programs for girls' education and children with disabilities.

These innovations aim to improve learning outcomes, reduce dropout rates, and make education inclusive and equitable.

Conclusion

The present status of primary education in India reflects significant achievements in access and enrollment, driven by policy reforms and government initiatives. However, challenges related to quality, infrastructure, teacher training, and equity require sustained attention. Implementing the goals of the NEP 2020, focusing on teacher professional development, enhancing infrastructure, and ensuring inclusive education can transform primary education into a strong foundation for India's future.

Practice Questions

A. Short Answer Questions

1. Define secondary education and explain its main characteristics.
2. What is the significance of secondary education in the overall educational system?
3. List and explain at least three aims of secondary education.
4. How does secondary education prepare students for higher education?
5. Mention two major challenges faced by secondary education in India.

B. Long Answer Questions

1. Discuss the concept and importance of secondary education in detail.
2. Explain the aims of secondary education and how they contribute to individual and societal development.
3. Analyse the role of secondary education in preparing students for future careers.
4. Evaluate the present status of secondary education in India and suggest measures for improvement.
5. Discuss the relationship between secondary education and social integration.

C. Multiple Choice Questions (MCQs)

1. Secondary education generally includes which grades?
   a) Grades 1–5
   b) Grades 6–12
   c) Grades 9–12
   d) Grades 1–8
2. One of the main aims of secondary education is:
   a) Providing only vocational skills
   b) Promoting holistic development
   c) Focusing solely on examination preparation
   d) Eliminating basic literacy teaching
3. Which of the following is NOT a feature of secondary education?
   a) Broad curriculum
   b) Specialized subject learning
   c) Focus on rote memorization only
   d) Preparation for higher education
4. What is the Gross Enrollment Ratio (GER) for secondary education in India approximately?
   a) 93%
   b) 77%
   c) 56%
   d) 100%

Chapter 7

Higher Education

1. Concept of Higher Education

Higher education refers to the stage of learning that follows the completion of secondary education. It is usually offered by universities, colleges, and professional institutions and includes undergraduate, postgraduate, and doctoral programs. Higher education aims to provide advanced knowledge, specialized skills, and research capabilities in diverse disciplines.

It includes formal programs such as bachelor's degrees, master's degrees, and doctoral studies, as well as professional and vocational education that prepares individuals for specific careers. Higher education is not limited to academic knowledge; it also fosters critical thinking, innovation, creativity, and ethical reasoning.

2. Aims of Higher Education

The aims of higher education are multi-dimensional, focusing on the intellectual, personal, social, and economic development of individuals and society. Some major aims include:

a) Development of Advanced Knowledge and Skills

Higher education aims to deepen knowledge in specific fields and develop professional and technical competencies.

b) Promotion of Research and Innovation

It fosters a research-oriented mindset, encouraging students and faculty to contribute to knowledge creation and innovation.

c) Preparation for Professional Careers

Higher education equips students with the skills, qualifications, and training required for professional employment.

d) Development of Critical Thinking and Problem-Solving Abilities

It encourages analytical thinking, independent judgment, and creative solutions to complex problems.

e) Enhancement of Personal Development

Higher education promotes maturity, self-discipline, moral values, and a sense of responsibility.

f) Promotion of Civic Responsibility

It cultivates a sense of citizenship, ethical behavior, and participation in societal development.

g) Fostering Global Competence

Higher education prepares students to operate effectively in a globalized world, emphasizing cross-cultural understanding and adaptability.

3. Importance of Higher Education

a) Economic Development

Higher education is critical for producing skilled professionals who contribute to the workforce, innovation, and economic growth. Knowledge-based economies rely heavily on highly educated individuals.

b) Social Transformation

Higher education promotes social mobility and helps reduce inequalities by providing opportunities for individuals to improve their status through knowledge and skills.

c) Cultural Enrichment

Higher education fosters cultural awareness, appreciation for diversity, and the preservation and transmission of cultural heritage.

d) Technological Advancement

Universities and research institutions are hubs for technological innovation, driving progress in science, engineering, medicine, and other fields.

e) Strengthening Democracy

Educated citizens are better equipped to participate in democratic processes, make informed decisions, and uphold democratic values.

f) Personal Growth

Higher education fosters intellectual curiosity, broadens perspectives, and encourages lifelong learning.

4. Higher Education in India: Current Scenario

India's higher education system is one of the largest in the world, comprising more than 1,000 universities and over 40,000 colleges. It offers a wide range of academic and professional courses, catering to diverse interests and career paths.

Key features of India's higher education system:

- Diverse disciplines and professional courses.
- Integration of technology and online learning.
- Research and innovation centres.
- International collaborations and student exchange programs.

Despite its scale, the system faces challenges such as quality gaps, inadequate research output, faculty shortages, and regional disparities in access to higher education.

5. Challenges in Higher Education

- **Quality and Accreditation**: Many institutions lack proper accreditation and quality assurance mechanisms.
- **Access and Equity**: Marginalized communities still face barriers to higher education.

- **Research Output**: Low levels of research innovation and publications compared to global standards.
- **Infrastructure Deficits**: Lack of modern facilities, laboratories, and libraries in some institutions.
- **Skill Gap**: Graduates often lack employable skills despite academic qualifications.

6. Importance of Reform in Higher Education

The **National Education Policy (NEP) 2020** proposes significant reforms to improve higher education in India:

- Multidisciplinary and holistic education.
- Integration of technology and digital learning.
- Emphasis on research and innovation.
- Increased autonomy for higher education institutions.
- Greater international collaboration.

These reforms aim to make higher education in India globally competitive, research-oriented, and inclusive.

7. Conclusion

Higher education plays a vital role in shaping the intellectual, professional, and ethical capacities of individuals. It is indispensable for the socio-economic and cultural development of society. By fulfilling its aims — advancing knowledge, fostering research, promoting civic responsibility, and preparing skilled professionals — higher education acts as a pillar for nation-building. Continuous reforms, innovation, and inclusivity are essential to realize the full potential of higher education in India and globally.

Types of Universities in India

India has a diverse higher education system that includes different types of universities. These universities differ in governance, funding, objectives, and scope. The main types of universities in India are **Central Universities**, **State Universities**, **Private Universities**, and **Open Universities**.

1. Central Universities

Definition

Central universities are institutions established by an Act of Parliament and are funded and managed by the Government of India through the Ministry of Education.

Features

- Funded primarily by the central government.
- Governed by the University Grants Commission (UGC).
- Have high academic standards and offer a wide range of courses.
- Often have national-level reputations for quality education and research.

Examples

Jawaharlal Nehru University (JNU), University of Delhi (DU), Banaras Hindu University (BHU), University of Hyderabad.

Importance

Central universities serve as models of academic excellence, provide opportunities for research, and often have diverse student populations representing various regions of India.

2. State Universities

Definition

State universities are established by Acts of the respective state legislatures and are funded and managed by state governments.

Features

- Funded by the respective state governments.
- Governed under the laws of the particular state.
- Often focus on serving the educational needs of the state's population.
- Affiliated colleges in the state are usually linked to a state university.

Examples

University of Calcutta (West Bengal), Osmania University (Telangana), Punjab University (Chandigarh), Banaras Hindu University (State-level affiliation in some courses).

Importance

State universities make higher education accessible at the regional level, cater to local needs, and promote cultural and linguistic diversity. They often offer education at lower costs compared to private institutions.

3. Private Universities

Definition

Private universities are established through state or central acts but are funded and managed by private organizations or trusts.

Features

- Funded and managed by private bodies such as trusts, societies, or companies.
- Have greater flexibility in curriculum design and management.
- Often charge higher fees compared to public universities.
- Offer specialized programs and industry-oriented courses.

Examples

Amity University, Manipal University, Shiv Nadar University, OP Jindal Global University.

Importance

Private universities provide alternatives to public education, often introducing innovation, modern infrastructure, and industry collaborations. They help in meeting the growing demand for higher education in India.

4. Open Universities

Definition

Open universities provide distance education, making higher education accessible to learners who cannot attend regular full-time courses.

Features

- Offer flexible learning through distance and online modes.
- Do not have strict eligibility criteria for admission.
- Provide a wide range of programs including certificates, diplomas, undergraduate, and postgraduate courses.
- Use technology extensively for teaching and assessment.

Examples

Indira Gandhi National Open University (IGNOU), Dr. B.R. Ambedkar Open University, Netaji Subhas Open University.

Importance

Open universities expand access to higher education for working adults, rural students, differently-abled learners, and those unable to attend regular classes due to personal or economic constraints. They promote lifelong learning and inclusivity.

Comparison Table

Type of University	Funding Source	Governance	Key Strengths	Examples
Central Universities	Central Government	UGC	High quality, diverse programs	JNU, DU, BHU
State Universities	State Government	State legislature	Regional focus, affordable fees	University of Calcutta, Osmania University

Private Universities	Private Bodies	State/Central Acts	Flexibility, innovation, infrastructure	Amity University, Manipal University
Open Universities	Government/Private	UGC	Flexibility, inclusivity, distance education	IGNOU, Dr. B.R. Ambedkar Open University

Conclusion

India's diverse higher education system ensures that students have multiple pathways to pursue higher learning. **Central and State Universities** ensure academic inclusivity and regional representation, **Private Universities** drive innovation and industry connections, and **Open Universities** extend learning opportunities beyond geographical and time boundaries. Each type of university plays a vital role in achieving the national goal of universal and quality higher education.

Present Status of Higher Education in India

1. Introduction

Higher education is a critical pillar of national development. It not only provides advanced knowledge and specialized skills but also fosters research, innovation, critical thinking, and civic responsibility. In India, higher education has witnessed tremendous expansion over the last few decades, both in terms of the number of institutions and student enrollment. However, despite significant growth, the system still faces multiple challenges related to quality, equity, infrastructure, employability, and research capacity.

This section provides a comprehensive analysis of the present status of higher education in India, examining the current structure, enrollment trends, quality issues, policy initiatives, challenges, and future directions.

2. Institutional Landscape

India's higher education system is one of the largest in the world. It comprises a variety of institutions, broadly categorized as:

- **Central Universities**: Established by Acts of Parliament and funded by the Central Government.
- **State Universities**: Established by state legislatures and funded by state governments.
- **Deemed-to-be Universities**: Granted autonomy for excellence in specific areas of study.
- **Private Universities**: Established and funded by private bodies or trusts.

- **Institutes of National Importance**: Prestigious institutions such as IITs, IIMs, AIIMS, which receive special funding and autonomy.
- **Colleges**: Offering undergraduate and postgraduate programs, affiliated with universities.

Statistics (2025):

- Over **1,000 universities** (including central, state, deemed, and private universities).
- Around **52,000+ colleges** spread across the country.
- More than **43 million students** enrolled in higher education.
- Over **1.6 million faculty members**, with more than 60% holding doctoral degrees.

This large structure enables diversity in academic offerings but also brings challenges of regulation, quality assurance, and uniformity.

3. Enrollment Trends

The **Gross Enrollment Ratio (GER)** is a key indicator of access to higher education. GER refers to the total enrollment in higher education as a percentage of the population in the relevant age group.

- **GER in India**: Around **33% in 2023**, up from 6% in 1995 — a remarkable achievement.
- **Total Enrollment**: Over **43.3 million students** in universities and colleges.

- Growth in enrollment is driven by demographic expansion, increased aspirations, and supportive government policies.

Gender and Regional Trends:

- Gender gap persists: GER for males is higher than for females, though female participation is increasing steadily.
- Regional variations: States like Tamil Nadu and Kerala have GERs above 40%, whereas Bihar, Uttar Pradesh, and Jharkhand lag behind, with GERs below 20%.
- Urban-rural gap: Students in urban areas have greater access due to better infrastructure and higher availability of institutions.

4. Quality of Higher Education

While access to higher education has expanded, quality remains a major concern.

Issues affecting quality:

- **Teacher Quality**: Shortages of qualified faculty, outdated teaching methods, and inadequate professional development opportunities affect learning outcomes.
- **Curriculum Relevance**: Many programs lack alignment with industry needs, reducing employability of graduates.
- **Infrastructure**: Some institutions, especially in rural areas, lack adequate classrooms, laboratories, libraries, and digital facilities.

- **Accreditation**: Not all universities and colleges maintain high standards; quality assurance mechanisms need strengthening.

Positive developments:

- Adoption of new pedagogies, blended learning, and digital resources.
- Introduction of multidisciplinary courses.
- Greater emphasis on research-oriented programs.

5. Research and Innovation

Research is the backbone of higher education, and India has been making efforts to strengthen its research ecosystem.

Current status:

- India's research output has been rising steadily, particularly in science, technology, medicine, and agriculture.
- However, global comparisons show India still trails in research publications per capita and patent generation.
- Funding constraints and limited collaboration between academia and industry hinder innovation.

Initiatives to promote research:

- Establishment of **Centers of Excellence** and research hubs.
- Increased funding through government schemes.

- Encouragement of interdisciplinary research under NEP 2020.

6. Policy Framework and Reforms

The Government of India has introduced several policies to strengthen higher education. The **National Education Policy (NEP) 2020** is a major reform with a vision to transform higher education.

Key features of NEP 2020:

- Multidisciplinary education and flexibility in course choices.
- Integration of technology in teaching, learning, and governance.
- Establishment of **multidisciplinary institutions** and higher education clusters.
- Increased autonomy for higher education institutions.
- Promotion of research and innovation through dedicated funding and support.
- Emphasis on Indian languages and cultural heritage.

NEP 2020 sets an ambitious target of achieving a **GER of 50% by 2035**.

7. Challenges in Higher Education

Despite progress, several challenges remain:

a) Quality and Accreditation

The variation in teaching quality across institutions is significant. Strengthening accreditation processes is critical for ensuring uniform standards.

b) Employability

Reports suggest that only about **50% of graduates** are employable. Bridging the gap between academic learning and industry requirements is a priority.

c) Access and Equity

Marginalized groups, women, and rural students still face barriers in accessing higher education. There is a need for scholarships, support programs, and outreach initiatives.

d) Research Funding

Research activities often suffer from limited funding and bureaucratic hurdles, restricting innovation.

e) Infrastructure Deficit

Many institutions still lack modern facilities such as digital classrooms, laboratories, libraries, and hostel accommodations.

8. Technological Integration

Technology is transforming higher education in India:

- Online learning platforms and MOOCs have expanded access.
- Digital classrooms, virtual labs, and AI-assisted teaching are becoming mainstream.
- E-libraries and open educational resources enhance learning opportunities.
- Technology also enables lifelong learning for working professionals.

9. Globalization and International Collaboration

Indian higher education is becoming more global:

- Increased student mobility and exchange programs.
- Partnerships with foreign universities for joint programs and research.
- Recognition of Indian degrees in several countries.
- International students contributing to India's education ecosystem.

Challenges include aligning curriculum with global standards and improving the international ranking of Indian institutions.

10. Future Directions

To strengthen higher education, India needs:

- Focus on quality assurance and accreditation.
- Greater industry-academia collaboration to improve employability.

- Expansion of research and innovation capabilities.
- Enhanced infrastructure, especially in rural areas.
- Bridging regional and gender disparities.
- Leveraging technology for teaching, learning, and administration.
- Encouraging lifelong learning and skill development.

Practice Questions

A. Short Answer Questions

1. Define the term "Higher Education" and explain its significance in national development.
2. What is the Gross Enrollment Ratio (GER) in India for higher education as of 2025?
3. Mention any two major challenges faced by higher education in India today.
4. What role does technology play in transforming higher education in India?
5. Name any two institutes of national importance in India and explain their importance.

B. Long Answer Questions

1. Analyse the present status of higher education in India with reference to institutional structure, enrollment trends, and quality issues.

2. Discuss the role of the National Education Policy (NEP) 2020 in reforming higher education in India.
3. Explain the challenges of access, equity, and employability in higher education in India.
4. Evaluate the present research and innovation ecosystem in India's higher education system.
5. Suggest measures to improve the quality and global competitiveness of higher education in India.

C. Multiple Choice Questions (MCQs)

1. Which of the following is the approximate Gross Enrollment Ratio (GER) for higher education in India in 2023?
   a) 20%
   b) 33%
   c) 45%
   d) 60%
2. Which policy framework has been introduced in India to reform higher education?
   a) RTE Act 2009
   b) NEP 2020
   c) NCF 2005
   d) Right to Education Policy
3. Institutes of National Importance in India include:
   a) IITs and IIMs
   b) Kendriya Vidyalayas
   c) Private Colleges only
   d) State Schools

4. One of the major aims of NEP 2020 is:
   a) Reducing higher education access
   b) Promoting multidisciplinary education
   c) Limiting research funding
   d) Removing technology from classrooms
5. Which state has the highest GER in India?
   a) Bihar
   b) Tamil Nadu
   c) Uttar Pradesh
   d) Jharkhand

Chapter 8

Guiding and Regulatory Bodies of Education in India

Ministry of Education (MHRD)

1. Introduction

The **Ministry of Education (MoE)**, formerly known as the **Ministry of Human Resource Development (MHRD)**, is a key government body in India responsible for the formulation and implementation of policies related to education in the country. In July 2020, MHRD was renamed the Ministry of Education to better reflect its role in promoting holistic education for all.

The Ministry oversees school education, higher education, literacy, vocational training, and educational reforms. It plays a central role in ensuring that education contributes to India's socio-economic development and aligns with global educational standards.

2. Objectives of the Ministry of Education

The main objectives of the Ministry of Education include:

- **Policy Formulation**: Designing policies for school and higher education in India.
- **Promotion of Quality Education**: Ensuring quality in teaching and learning at all levels.
- **Skill Development**: Promoting vocational and skill-based education to enhance employability.

- **Research and Innovation**: Encouraging research, innovation, and multidisciplinary education.
- **Equitable Access**: Ensuring access to education for all sections of society, including marginalized communities.
- **International Cooperation**: Building partnerships with other countries and international organizations in education.

3. Structure of the Ministry

The Ministry of Education has two main departments:

1. **Department of School Education and Literacy** – responsible for primary, secondary, and adult education.
2. **Department of Higher Education** – responsible for universities, colleges, technical education, and research.

It also oversees various autonomous bodies and institutions such as:

- University Grants Commission (UGC)
- All India Council for Technical Education (AICTE)
- National Council of Educational Research and Training (NCERT)
- Kendriya Vidyalaya Sangathan (KVS)
- Navodaya Vidyalaya Samiti (NVS)
- Indira Gandhi National Open University (IGNOU)

4. Key Initiatives and Programs

The Ministry of Education has launched several initiatives to improve the quality, reach, and accessibility of education:

a) National Education Policy (NEP) 2020

The NEP aims to transform India's education system by promoting multidisciplinary learning, flexibility in course choices, integration of technology, and research orientation.

b) SWAYAM

An online platform providing free courses for school and higher education students, enabling open access to quality learning resources.

c) National Digital Education Architecture (NDEAR)

Aims to create a digital ecosystem to improve access and quality in education across India.

d) Skill India Mission

Focuses on enhancing vocational training and skill development for employability.

e) Samagra Shiksha Abhiyan

Integrates various programs for school education to improve quality and ensure inclusive education.

5. Importance of the Ministry of Education

The Ministry is central to shaping India's educational landscape. It determines the direction of educational reforms, ensures equitable access, and promotes research and innovation. It is instrumental in achieving national development goals by empowering individuals through quality education and skills.

UNESCO (United Nations Educational, Scientific and Cultural Organization)

1. Introduction

UNESCO stands for the **United Nations Educational, Scientific and Cultural Organization**. It is a specialized agency of the United Nations established on **16 November 1945** with the aim of promoting peace and security through international collaboration in education, science, culture, and communication. UNESCO's headquarters is located in Paris, France.

The organization works to foster intercultural dialogue, sustainable development, and quality education for all, and it plays a key role in addressing global challenges in education, science, culture, and communication.

2. Objectives of UNESCO

The primary objectives of UNESCO are:

- **Promotion of Education**: To ensure inclusive and equitable quality education and promote lifelong learning opportunities for all.

- **Scientific Advancement**: To encourage international cooperation in the fields of science and technology.
- **Cultural Preservation**: To protect cultural heritage and promote cultural diversity.
- **Freedom of Expression**: To promote freedom of expression and access to information.
- **Sustainable Development**: To support education, science, and culture as means for sustainable development and peace.

3. Structure of UNESCO

UNESCO is composed of:

1. **The General Conference** – The main decision-making body where member states meet every two years.
2. **The Executive Board** – Responsible for ensuring that UNESCO's policies and programs are implemented.
3. **The Secretariat** – Headed by the Director-General, which carries out the day-to-day work of UNESCO.

UNESCO currently has **193 member states** and **11 associate members**, making it a truly global organization.

4. Key Programs and Initiatives of UNESCO

a) Education for Sustainable Development (ESD)

Promotes integrating sustainability principles into education at all levels to prepare learners for a sustainable future.

b) Education 2030 Framework

Aligned with the United Nations' Sustainable Development Goal 4 (SDG 4), which aims to "ensure inclusive and equitable quality education and promote lifelong learning opportunities for all."

c) Global Education Monitoring (GEM) Report

Provides annual monitoring of progress towards global education goals and policies.

d) Cultural Heritage Protection

UNESCO's World Heritage Sites program identifies and preserves places of cultural and natural significance worldwide.

e) Science and Technology Programs

Encourages research collaboration, knowledge sharing, and capacity building in science and technology fields.

5. UNESCO's Role in India

India has been a member of UNESCO since 1946. UNESCO collaborates with India in:

- Promoting quality education and literacy programs.
- Preserving cultural heritage, including monuments and intangible heritage.

- Supporting scientific research and environmental sustainability.
- Encouraging digital and distance education.

Examples include projects under UNESCO's **Global Education Monitoring** and collaborations on cultural preservation, such as the preservation of monuments like the Taj Mahal.

6. Importance of UNESCO

UNESCO plays a vital role in fostering international cooperation in education, science, culture, and communication. It helps member states build policies and frameworks that ensure quality education, protect cultural diversity, and promote sustainable development. UNESCO serves as a platform for dialogue and collaboration among nations to address global educational and cultural challenges.

NCERT (National Council of Educational Research and Training)

1. Introduction

The **National Council of Educational Research and Training (NCERT)** is an autonomous organisation established by the Government of India in **1961**. Its primary objective is to assist and advise the central and state governments on academic matters related to school education. NCERT plays a vital role in the development of curriculum frameworks, textbooks, and educational research in India.

Headquartered in New Delhi, NCERT functions under the Ministry of Education (MoE) and is one of the most important institutions in the Indian education system.

2. Objectives of NCERT

NCERT aims to:

- Develop and revise curricula and syllabi for school education.
- Publish textbooks and other learning materials for school students.
- Conduct educational research and promote innovation in teaching methods.
- Provide training and resources for teachers and educators.
- Support state educational departments in implementing educational reforms.

3. Structure of NCERT

NCERT is governed by a General Council, which is headed by the Union Minister of Education and includes representatives from various states and territories. The organisation is divided into several divisions and centres specializing in curriculum development, teacher training, research, and publication.

Key divisions include:

- Curriculum and Syllabus Division
- Educational Technology Division

- Teacher Education Division
- Publication Division
- Research and Innovation Division

4. Key Functions of NCERT

a) Curriculum Development

NCERT develops frameworks for school education, including the **National Curriculum Framework (NCF)**, which provides guidelines for syllabus design and teaching strategies.

b) Textbook Publication

NCERT publishes textbooks for classes I to XII, widely used in CBSE schools and state education boards. These textbooks are designed to ensure conceptual clarity, inclusivity, and quality education.

c) Teacher Training

NCERT organises training programs, workshops, and seminars for teachers to improve their teaching skills and professional competence.

d) Educational Research

It conducts studies and research in education to suggest improvements in curriculum design, teaching methodology, and learning assessment.

e) Innovation in Education

NCERT promotes innovative teaching methods, including the use of ICT, project-based learning, and experiential learning practices.

5. NCERT and the National Education Policy (NEP) 2020

NCERT plays a key role in implementing NEP 2020 by:

- Revising curriculum frameworks to promote multidisciplinary education.
- Developing textbooks that integrate contemporary knowledge and skill-based learning.
- Supporting teacher training aligned with NEP objectives.
- Encouraging the use of technology in teaching and learning.

6. Importance of NCERT

NCERT serves as a backbone of school education in India. Its textbooks and curriculum frameworks ensure quality, standardisation, and equity in education. The organisation bridges the gap between educational policy and classroom practice by providing teacher training, research insights, and resource materials.

SCERT (State Council of Educational Research and Training)

1. Introduction

The **State Council of Educational Research and Training (SCERT)** is an autonomous body established by the respective state governments in India. SCERT acts as the apex resource centre for school education in each state. It is responsible for academic planning, curriculum development, teacher education, and educational research at the state level.

SCERT plays a crucial role in implementing national educational policies such as the **National Education Policy (NEP) 2020** within the context of each state's specific requirements, culture, and linguistic diversity.

2. Objectives of SCERT

The main objectives of SCERT include:

- Development and revision of state-level curricula and syllabi.
- Preparation of textbooks, teaching-learning materials, and educational resources.
- Conducting training programs for teachers and teacher educators.
- Promoting educational research and innovation.
- Advising the state government on policy matters related to education.
- Supporting the implementation of national education policies and programmes at the state level.

3. Structure of SCERT

Each SCERT is governed by a governing body that includes representatives from the state education department, universities, and academic experts. SCERT generally consists of several divisions and cells, such as:

- Curriculum Development Division
- Teacher Education Division
- Research and Evaluation Division
- Educational Technology Division
- Textbook and Publication Division

The organisation works closely with District Institutes of Education and Training (DIETs) and other teacher training institutes to improve school education quality.

4. Functions of SCERT

a) Curriculum Development

SCERT is responsible for developing and revising the curriculum and syllabus in accordance with the National Curriculum Framework (NCF) and the needs of the state. It ensures that curricula reflect the cultural, linguistic, and regional diversity of the state while maintaining national standards.

b) Teacher Training

SCERT organises pre-service and in-service teacher training programmes. These programs aim to enhance teachers' professional competence, introduce innovative teaching methods, and integrate technology in teaching.

c) Textbook Preparation

SCERT prepares and publishes textbooks and supplementary materials in the regional language, which are aligned with the curriculum. These materials are often adapted to local needs and contexts.

d) Research and Innovation

SCERT conducts educational research to improve teaching-learning processes, curriculum design, and assessment methods. It also experiments with innovative pedagogical strategies.

e) Educational Support and Guidance

SCERT provides academic support to schools and teacher training institutes, monitors educational programmes, and evaluates their effectiveness.

5. SCERT and NEP 2020

SCERT is central to implementing NEP 2020 at the state level by:

- Revising state curricula to promote multidisciplinary and holistic education.
- Developing textbooks that incorporate experiential learning and skill development.
- Strengthening teacher training programmes in line with NEP guidelines.
- Promoting the use of ICT and digital learning resources in education.

6. Importance of SCERT

SCERT serves as the backbone of state-level education planning and reform. It ensures that educational policies are adapted to the specific needs of states and translates national-level policies into practical action at the local level. SCERT acts as a bridge between policy-making bodies like NCERT and the grassroots education system.

DIET (District Institute of Education and Training)

1. Introduction

The **District Institute of Education and Training (DIET)** is a key institution in India's elementary education system, established under the **National Policy on Education (1986)** and operationalised after 1992. DIETs function at the district level to improve the quality of elementary education by focusing on teacher training, curriculum support, and educational research.

DIETs serve as academic and resource centres to support the entire school education system in their respective districts. They act as a link between state-level training institutions such as SCERT and grassroots school education.

2. Objectives of DIET

The main objectives of DIET are:

- To provide pre-service and in-service training to elementary school teachers.
- To develop curriculum-based teaching-learning materials.
- To provide academic support to schools and teachers.
- To conduct action research and educational innovation at the district level.
- To strengthen the capacity of teachers and teacher educators.
- To support the implementation of national and state education policies at the district level.

3. Structure of DIET

DIETs generally have a hierarchical structure comprising:

- **Principal**: Academic head of the institute.
- **Teacher Educators**: Subject specialists for different areas of elementary education.
- **Resource Persons**: Experts for special programmes and training.
- Administrative and support staff.

DIET functions through various specialized cells or divisions such as:

- Curriculum and Material Development Cell
- Teacher Education Cell
- Educational Research and Evaluation Cell
- Extension and Support Cell

4. Functions of DIET

a) Teacher Education

DIET provides both pre-service training for prospective elementary school teachers and in-service training for serving teachers. Training programmes include workshops, seminars, and capacity-building courses aimed at improving teaching effectiveness.

b) Curriculum Support

DIET works to adapt and contextualize the curriculum developed by NCERT and SCERT for the district level. This includes the preparation of teaching aids, supplementary materials, and learning resources for school students.

c) Research and Innovation

DIET conducts action research and pilot projects to develop innovative teaching methods and assessment strategies for elementary education.

d) Academic Support to Schools

DIETs provide guidance to schools in implementing curriculum reforms, pedagogical strategies, and innovative teaching methods. They also monitor and evaluate school performance.

e) Community Participation

DIET promotes the involvement of community members, parents, and local bodies in improving the quality of elementary education.

5. DIET and National Education Policy (NEP) 2020

DIETs play an important role in implementing NEP 2020 at the grassroots level:

- Organising training for teachers on multidisciplinary and experiential learning approaches.
- Integrating digital and ICT-based teaching methodologies.
- Supporting schools in adopting competency-based education and new assessment methods.
- Encouraging community engagement in the educational process.

6. Importance of DIET

DIET is a cornerstone of teacher education and capacity building in India. By working at the district level, it ensures that educational policies and curriculum reforms are implemented effectively. DIET acts as a bridge between policy-making bodies and schools, ensuring that quality education reaches all students, especially in rural and remote areas.

NIOS (National Institute of Open Schooling)

1. Introduction

The **National Institute of Open Schooling (NIOS)** is an autonomous institution under the Ministry of Education, Government of India. It was established in **1989** as the **National Open School** and was later renamed NIOS in 2002. NIOS provides flexible learning opportunities to learners who cannot pursue formal education through regular schools.

NIOS aims to democratize education by making learning accessible to all, especially disadvantaged groups such as working adults, rural learners, dropouts, and differently-abled students. It is the largest open schooling system in the world.

2. Objectives of NIOS

The key objectives of NIOS are:

- To provide education to all learners, including those outside the formal schooling system.
- To offer flexible curricula and examination systems for learners with different needs and backgrounds.
- To promote lifelong learning opportunities.
- To develop quality instructional materials and digital resources for learners.

- To ensure inclusive education for marginalized and disadvantaged groups.

3. Structure of NIOS

NIOS operates through a network of:

- **Headquarters** in Noida, Uttar Pradesh.
- **Regional Centres** across India to manage enrolment, learner support, and administration.
- **Study Centres** and accredited institutions providing guidance and facilitation for learners.

The governance of NIOS includes an Executive Committee and Academic Committees responsible for policy decisions, curriculum development, and examination regulations.

4. Key Functions of NIOS

a) Secondary and Senior Secondary Education

NIOS offers courses equivalent to Class X (Secondary) and Class XII (Senior Secondary) in academic and vocational streams, providing flexibility in subject choice and examination schedules.

b) Vocational Education

NIOS offers a variety of vocational courses designed to enhance employability skills. These courses are tailored to meet the needs of industry and society.

c) Teacher Training

NIOS conducts teacher training programmes to promote open and distance learning methods and improve the quality of education delivery.

d) Curriculum and Study Material Development

NIOS develops textbooks, audio-video materials, and e-learning resources to facilitate self-paced learning.

e) Examination and Certification

NIOS conducts examinations twice a year and awards certificates recognized nationally and internationally.

5. Features of NIOS

- Flexible admission process without rigid age limits.
- Choice-based credit system allowing learners to choose subjects.
- On-demand examination system for certain courses.
- Use of technology through online courses, e-content, and virtual classrooms.
- Inclusive approach, catering to differently-abled learners and those in remote areas.

6. Importance of NIOS

NIOS plays a crucial role in increasing access to education for disadvantaged and non-traditional learners. It enables lifelong learning, promotes skill development, and addresses the needs of learners who cannot attend regular schools due to economic, social, or geographical constraints. NIOS helps in bridging gaps in education and supports the vision of inclusive education outlined in the National Education Policy (NEP) 2020.

7. NIOS and NEP 2020

Under NEP 2020, NIOS is expected to play an important role in:

- Expanding open and distance learning as a viable alternative to formal schooling.
- Providing skill-based and vocational education aligned with employability requirements.
- Integrating digital learning and technology in its educational delivery.
- Promoting inclusive education for disadvantaged learners.

NUEPA (National University of Educational Planning and Administration)

1. Introduction

The **National University of Educational Planning and Administration (NUEPA)** is an autonomous institution established by the Government of India in **1988**. NUEPA functions as a premier research and training institution in the fields of educational planning, policy formulation, management, and administration. It operates under the Ministry of Education, Government of India, and plays a vital role in shaping educational governance and reforms in the country.

NUEPA is headquartered in New Delhi and focuses on capacity building, research, policy analysis, and advisory services to improve the quality and accessibility of education in India.

2. Objectives of NUEPA

The main objectives of NUEPA are:

- To build capacities of education planners, administrators, and managers.
- To undertake research in the fields of educational planning, policy, and administration.
- To develop and disseminate innovative approaches in education management.
- To support policy formulation and implementation at national and state levels.
- To promote quality improvement in educational governance.

3. Structure of NUEPA

NUEPA is governed by a General Council and an Executive Council comprising education experts, government representatives, and academic leaders. It is structured into several centres and divisions specializing in:

- Educational Planning
- Educational Management and Administration
- Research and Policy Analysis
- Capacity Building and Training
- Educational Information and Data Analysis

NUEPA collaborates with central and state governments, universities, and international organisations to enhance educational governance.

4. Key Functions of NUEPA

a) Capacity Building and Training

NUEPA organises training programmes, workshops, and courses for educational planners, administrators, and policy makers at central, state, and district levels. These programmes aim to enhance efficiency and effectiveness in educational governance.

b) Research and Policy Studies

NUEPA conducts research on issues related to educational planning, policy reforms, financing, quality improvement, equity, and governance. Its research outputs contribute to informed decision-making in education.

c) Educational Planning and Management

The university provides technical support and consultancy to central and state governments in the preparation of educational plans, programmes, and policy documents.

d) Data Collection and Analysis

NUEPA collects, compiles, and analyses educational data to monitor the progress of educational initiatives and to identify challenges and opportunities for improvement.

e) Publication and Dissemination

NUEPA publishes research reports, policy briefs, manuals, and journals such as the **Journal of Educational Planning and Administration** to share knowledge and best practices in the field.

5. NUEPA and NEP 2020

Under the **National Education Policy (NEP) 2020**, NUEPA is expected to play a crucial role in:

- Strengthening capacities of educational administrators and planners.
- Providing policy inputs for implementing NEP initiatives.
- Promoting evidence-based decision-making through research and data analysis.
- Supporting systemic reforms in governance and administration of education.

6. Importance of NUEPA

NUEPA is a vital institution in India's education system. It ensures effective planning, management, and governance of educational programmes. NUEPA's research and capacity-building initiatives help policy makers and administrators design and implement educational reforms that align with national goals and international standards.

NCTE (National Council for Teacher Education)

1. Introduction

The **National Council for Teacher Education (NCTE)** is a statutory body established in **1993** under the National Council for Teacher Education Act, 1993. It functions under the Ministry of Education, Government of India, with the primary responsibility of ensuring the proper planning and coordinated development of the teacher education system in the country.

NCTE plays a key role in improving the quality of teacher education and setting standards for teacher preparation institutions in India.

2. Objectives of NCTE

The main objectives of NCTE are:

- To achieve planned and coordinated development of the teacher education system.

- To regulate and maintain norms and standards in teacher education institutions.
- To ensure the quality and relevance of teacher education programmes.
- To promote research and innovation in teacher education.
- To prepare competent and professional teachers for elementary, secondary, and higher education.

3. Structure of NCTE

NCTE is governed by a Governing Body headed by a Chairperson. The council comprises experts from the fields of education, government representatives, and members nominated by the central and state governments.

Its structure includes several regional committees and sub-committees that address different aspects of teacher education, such as curriculum development, accreditation, and quality monitoring.

4. Functions of NCTE

a) Norms and Standards

NCTE lays down the norms and standards for teacher education programmes and institutions across the country. These include curriculum frameworks, admission criteria, teacher-student ratios, faculty qualifications, and infrastructural requirements.

b) Accreditation and Recognition

NCTE is responsible for granting recognition to teacher education institutions and periodically reviewing their performance to ensure compliance with prescribed standards.

c) Curriculum Development

NCTE develops model curricula and guidelines for various teacher education programmes such as B.Ed., D.El.Ed., M.Ed., and integrated teacher training courses.

d) Quality Monitoring

The council monitors teacher education institutions to ensure that they maintain high-quality teaching, research, and training practices.

e) Research and Innovation

NCTE encourages research in teacher education, innovative teaching methods, and the integration of technology in teacher preparation.

5. NCTE and National Education Policy (NEP) 2020

Under NEP 2020, NCTE is expected to play a crucial role in transforming teacher education by:

- Revising and restructuring teacher education curricula to promote multidisciplinary learning.
- Integrating technology and ICT in teacher education.

- Enhancing the quality of teacher preparation through continuous professional development.
- Encouraging research and innovation in teacher education pedagogy.

6. Importance of NCTE

NCTE is essential for maintaining quality and standardisation in teacher education in India. It ensures that teachers are well-prepared to meet the diverse needs of learners and the evolving requirements of the education system. By regulating teacher training institutions and curricula, NCTE safeguards the quality of education in the country.

UGC (University Grants Commission)

1. Introduction

The **University Grants Commission (UGC)** is a statutory body established in **1956** under the UGC Act, 1956. It operates under the Ministry of Education, Government of India, and serves as the apex body responsible for coordinating, determining, and maintaining standards of higher education in India.

UGC plays a crucial role in shaping the higher education system, ensuring quality, promoting research, and providing financial support to universities and colleges across the country.

2. Objectives of UGC

The main objectives of the UGC are:

- To coordinate and maintain standards of higher education in India.
- To promote and fund universities and higher education institutions.
- To support and promote research and innovation.
- To ensure academic freedom and autonomy in higher education institutions.
- To facilitate the integration of higher education with national development needs.

3. Structure of UGC

UGC is governed by a Commission consisting of a Chairperson and members appointed by the Government of India. Its structure includes several standing committees and departments for academic planning, funding, quality assurance, and research promotion.

UGC works in collaboration with universities, regulatory bodies, and other educational institutions to implement higher education policies effectively.

4. Functions of UGC

a) Funding and Grants

UGC provides financial assistance to universities and colleges for infrastructure development, research projects, and faculty development programmes. It allocates grants for special projects and promotes innovation in teaching and learning.

b) Standard Setting and Accreditation

UGC prescribes and maintains academic standards in universities and colleges. It works with accreditation agencies such as NAAC (National Assessment and Accreditation Council) to ensure quality assurance.

c) Curriculum Development

UGC supports universities in developing and revising curricula to make them relevant to contemporary needs and global standards.

d) Promotion of Research

UGC encourages research by providing grants, scholarships, and fellowships to students and researchers. It also supports research centres and promotes interdisciplinary studies.

e) Policy Formulation

UGC plays a significant role in formulating policies for higher education and ensuring their implementation in coordination with state and central governments.

5. UGC and National Education Policy (NEP) 2020

Under NEP 2020, UGC is tasked with:

- Restructuring higher education institutions into multidisciplinary universities and colleges.
- Promoting research and innovation across disciplines.
- Strengthening quality assurance mechanisms.
- Encouraging autonomy in academic and administrative functions of universities.
- Facilitating the use of technology in higher education through digital initiatives.

6. Importance of UGC

UGC is the cornerstone of India's higher education system. It plays a pivotal role in ensuring academic excellence, funding research, and maintaining standards. UGC acts as a bridge between policy-making and institutional execution, ensuring that higher education in India is relevant, inclusive, and of high quality.

NAAC (National Assessment and Accreditation Council)

1. Introduction

The **National Assessment and Accreditation Council (NAAC)** is an autonomous institution established by the **University Grants Commission (UGC)** in **1994**. NAAC is headquartered in Bengaluru, Karnataka, and its primary objective is to assess and accredit higher education institutions in India to ensure and enhance quality in education.

NAAC plays a crucial role in improving the standards of higher education by promoting quality assurance and continuous improvement in teaching, research, and institutional functioning.

2. Objectives of NAAC

The main objectives of NAAC are:

- To promote quality assurance and improvement in higher education institutions.
- To assess and accredit universities and colleges based on defined quality parameters.
- To stimulate self-evaluation and accountability among higher education institutions.
- To encourage the adoption of best practices in teaching, learning, and administration.
- To promote innovation and research in higher education.

3. Structure of NAAC

NAAC is governed by a General Council, an Executive Committee, and various expert committees. The council comprises academicians, government representatives, and education experts. NAAC functions through a well-defined process of institutional assessment and accreditation involving peer teams and self-study reports.

4. Functions of NAAC

a) Accreditation of Institutions

NAAC assesses and accredits higher education institutions (universities and colleges) based on a comprehensive set of criteria. Accreditation is valid for a specified period after which institutions must apply for re-accreditation.

b) Quality Assurance Framework

NAAC develops quality benchmarks and assessment criteria that guide institutions in their quality improvement processes.

c) Capacity Building

NAAC organises workshops, seminars, and training programmes to build the capacity of higher education institutions in quality assurance and enhancement.

d) Research and Innovation Promotion

NAAC encourages research in quality assurance and accreditation processes, providing guidance to institutions for adopting innovative educational practices.

e) Publication and Dissemination

NAAC publishes reports, manuals, and guidelines related to quality assurance and accreditation, serving as a resource for higher education institutions.

5. NAAC Accreditation Process

The NAAC accreditation process includes:

1. **Institutional Information Submission** – Institutions submit self-study reports.
2. **Peer Team Visit** – Experts visit the institution to verify information.
3. **Evaluation** – Institutions are evaluated based on seven criteria including curricular aspects, teaching-learning processes, research, infrastructure, student support, governance, and innovation.
4. **Grading** – Institutions are graded on a scale ranging from A++ to D, where A++ denotes the highest quality.

6. NAAC and NEP 2020

Under the **National Education Policy (NEP) 2020**, NAAC is expected to:

- Revise accreditation processes to align with NEP's focus on multidisciplinary, holistic education.
- Promote continuous internal quality assurance mechanisms in institutions.
- Strengthen the use of technology and data analytics in quality assessment.
- Support institutions in aligning with global standards of quality higher education.

7. Importance of NAAC

NAAC is a cornerstone of quality assurance in Indian higher education. Accreditation by NAAC enhances the credibility of institutions, helps them identify areas for improvement, and strengthens accountability. NAAC plays a vital role in promoting academic excellence and aligning Indian higher education with international quality standards.

IQAC (Internal Quality Assurance Cell)

1. Introduction

The **Internal Quality Assurance Cell (IQAC)** is an essential component of higher education institutions in India, established following the recommendations of the **National Assessment and**

Accreditation Council (NAAC). IQAC was made mandatory for all higher education institutions seeking accreditation under NAAC guidelines.

The main objective of IQAC is to develop a system for conscious, consistent, and catalytic improvement in the overall performance of institutions. IQAC acts as a quality benchmark for academic and administrative processes.

2. Objectives of IQAC

The key objectives of IQAC are:

- To develop and apply quality benchmarks for various academic and administrative activities.
- To facilitate quality enhancement measures in higher education institutions.
- To promote internalization of quality culture in every aspect of the institution.
- To foster a learner-centric environment for quality education and faculty development.
- To build capacities for innovation and research.

3. Structure of IQAC

IQAC is generally headed by a senior faculty member, often designated as the Coordinator, and comprises representatives from:

- Teaching staff
- Administrative staff

- Students
- Alumni
- Employers and industry representatives
- Local community members

The size and structure of IQAC may vary depending on the size and nature of the institution, but it usually functions as a standing body responsible for quality assurance.

4. Functions of IQAC

a) Development and Application of Quality Benchmarks

IQAC develops quality benchmarks for various academic and administrative activities, ensuring continuous improvement in institutional performance.

b) Facilitating Quality Enhancement

It identifies institutional weaknesses and suggests measures for improvement. IQAC coordinates activities for curriculum design, teaching-learning processes, research, and governance.

c) Promoting Quality Culture

IQAC works to integrate quality consciousness into the institutional culture through workshops, seminars, and training programmes.

d) Documentation and Dissemination

It maintains records of quality assurance processes and prepares the Annual Quality Assurance Report (AQAR) for submission to NAAC.

e) Collaboration and Research

IQAC encourages collaborative initiatives and research activities that contribute to quality improvement.

5. IQAC and NAAC Accreditation

NAAC emphasises the role of IQAC in sustaining quality education. IQAC acts as an internal mechanism for quality assurance and plays a crucial role in:

- Preparing institutions for accreditation and re-accreditation.
- Ensuring compliance with NAAC's quality parameters.
- Coordinating quality-related activities across departments.

6. Importance of IQAC

IQAC is vital for continuous improvement in higher education institutions. It serves as the backbone for quality assurance, helping institutions align with national and international quality standards. IQAC strengthens the institution's capacity to achieve its vision and mission effectively.

7. IQAC and NEP 2020

Under the **National Education Policy (NEP) 2020**, IQAC's role is expected to expand to:

- Integrating holistic, multidisciplinary, and skill-oriented approaches in higher education.
- Promoting the use of ICT and digital tools for quality assurance.
- Facilitating innovations in curriculum design and teaching-learning methodologies.
- Encouraging participatory governance and stakeholder engagement.

AICTE (All India Council for Technical Education)

1. Introduction

The **All India Council for Technical Education (AICTE)** is a statutory body established in **1987** under the Ministry of Education, Government of India. AICTE is responsible for proper planning, coordination, and development of technical education and management education in India.

AICTE plays a pivotal role in ensuring quality, promoting innovation, and regulating technical and management institutions across the country.

2. Objectives of AICTE

The key objectives of AICTE are:

- To ensure coordinated and integrated development of technical education in India.
- To maintain norms and standards in technical and management education.
- To promote quality and excellence in technical education institutions.
- To support research and innovation in technical education.
- To facilitate access to technical education for all sections of society.

3. Structure of AICTE

AICTE is governed by a Council headed by a Chairman, with members nominated from central and state governments, industry, and academia. The council functions through various committees, including:

- Academic Committee
- Accreditation Committee
- Finance Committee
- Planning and Development Committee

AICTE operates through its regional offices to oversee implementation of its policies and regulations across India.

4. Functions of AICTE

a) Regulation and Accreditation

AICTE lays down norms and standards for technical and management education programmes. It grants approval to institutions offering these programmes and accredits them to ensure quality.

b) Curriculum Development

AICTE prepares model curricula for technical and management courses and encourages innovative approaches to teaching-learning.

c) Funding and Support

AICTE provides financial assistance for research projects, faculty development programmes, industry-institute collaborations, and infrastructure development.

d) Promotion of Research and Innovation

AICTE promotes research, innovation, and entrepreneurship in technical education through initiatives such as research grants, incubation centres, and innovation awards.

e) Quality Assurance

AICTE monitors compliance with established norms and standards through periodic inspections and reviews of technical institutions.

5. AICTE and National Education Policy (NEP) 2020

Under NEP 2020, AICTE is expected to:

- Promote multidisciplinary and holistic education in technical institutions.
- Strengthen industry-institute collaboration for skill development and employability.
- Support innovation, research, and entrepreneurship in technical education.
- Facilitate integration of digital learning and online education.
- Ensure equitable access to quality technical education.

6. Importance of AICTE

AICTE is a key institution in shaping the technical education landscape of India. By setting norms, ensuring quality, promoting innovation, and facilitating research, AICTE contributes to the advancement of technical education. It plays a significant role in preparing skilled professionals who contribute to national development and technological progress.

International Boards of Education

1. Introduction

International Boards of Education are educational authorities that design curricula, set academic standards, conduct examinations, and award qualifications that are recognised internationally. These boards operate across different countries and offer programmes in primary, secondary, and higher secondary education. They provide globally recognised qualifications and ensure consistency in quality education.

International Boards aim to promote global mobility of students, standardisation of education, and preparation for higher studies in various countries. They play a critical role in fostering intercultural understanding and global perspectives in education.

2. Objectives of International Boards

The main objectives of International Boards include:

- To provide high-quality education that is globally recognised.
- To ensure uniform academic standards across different countries and institutions.
- To promote holistic development of learners through diverse curricular and co-curricular activities.
- To prepare students for higher education and careers internationally.
- To encourage critical thinking, problem-solving, and intercultural competence.

3. Examples of Major International Boards

Some of the most prominent international boards include:

a) International Baccalaureate (IB)

Founded in 1968, IB offers programmes for students aged 3–19, focusing on intellectual, personal, emotional, and social growth. The main programmes are the Primary Years Programme (PYP), Middle Years Programme (MYP), and Diploma Programme (DP).

b) Cambridge Assessment International Education (CAIE)

CAIE, based in the UK, offers internationally recognised qualifications such as IGCSE and A-Levels. The curriculum emphasises analytical thinking, creativity, and global perspectives.

c) Council for the Indian School Certificate Examinations (CISCE)

CISCE is an Indian-based board offering the ICSE (Class 10) and ISC (Class 12) examinations with a broad and balanced curriculum.

d) International General Certificate of Secondary Education (IGCSE)

Offered by Cambridge, IGCSE is recognised worldwide for its academic rigor and flexibility.

e) Edexcel

Edexcel, part of Pearson, offers academic and vocational qualifications including GCSEs and A-Levels, recognised globally.

4. Key Features of International Boards

- **Global Recognition:** Certificates are accepted by universities and employers worldwide.
- **Flexible Curriculum:** Emphasis on broad learning and flexibility in subject choices.
- **Innovative Assessment:** Continuous assessment along with final examinations.
- **Holistic Development:** Focus on extracurricular activities, critical thinking, and creativity.
- **Multicultural Perspective:** Curriculum designed to foster global awareness and intercultural understanding.

5. Importance of International Boards

International Boards provide education that equips students with global competencies. They prepare learners to adapt to diverse academic and cultural environments, fostering skills like communication, problem-solving, and research. Their emphasis on high academic standards and holistic development ensures students are well-prepared for higher education and professional careers anywhere in the world.

6. Challenges Faced by International Boards

- Higher cost of education compared to national boards.
- Accessibility issues for students from rural and economically weaker backgrounds.
- Need for trained teachers familiar with international pedagogies.

- Balancing global standards with local cultural and educational contexts.

National Boards of Education

1. Introduction

National Boards of Education are government-recognised educational authorities that design and regulate school curricula, conduct examinations, and award certifications within a country. In India, national boards set academic standards to ensure consistency and quality in school education and to prepare students for higher education and national-level competitive examinations.

National boards focus on developing curricula that meet the country's cultural, social, and economic needs, while also promoting holistic education and national integration.

2. Objectives of National Boards

The main objectives of National Boards include:

- To establish uniform academic standards across schools in the country.
- To ensure accessibility of quality education to all students.
- To promote comprehensive development through academic and co-curricular programmes.

- To prepare students for higher education and employability in the national context.
- To promote cultural heritage, national values, and citizenship education.

3. Examples of Major National Boards in India

India has several prominent national boards that regulate school education:

a) CBSE (Central Board of Secondary Education)

- Established in 1962.
- Offers curriculum from primary to senior secondary level.
- Known for its structured curriculum and emphasis on Science, Mathematics, and English.
- Conducts All India Secondary School Examination (AISSE) for Class 10 and All India Senior School Certificate Examination (AISSCE) for Class 12.

b) CISCE (Council for the Indian School Certificate Examinations)

- Established in 1958.
- Conducts Indian Certificate of Secondary Education (ICSE) for Class 10 and Indian School Certificate (ISC) for Class 12.
- Known for its broad and balanced curriculum and emphasis on English proficiency.

c) State Education Boards

- Each state in India has its own board, e.g., Maharashtra State Board, Tamil Nadu State Board.
- Designs curricula relevant to regional languages, culture, and needs.
- Conducts state-level secondary and higher secondary examinations.

d) NIOS (National Institute of Open Schooling)

- Established in 1989.
- Provides flexible learning options for school education through open and distance learning.
- Offers secondary and senior secondary level education with flexibility in subjects and examination schedules.

4. Key Features of National Boards

- **Uniform Curriculum:** Standardised syllabi ensure consistency in academic content.
- **National Relevance:** Curricula align with the socio-cultural and economic priorities of the country.
- **Inclusive Education:** Provision for students from diverse socio-economic backgrounds.
- **Cultural and Value Education:** Emphasis on Indian culture, heritage, and constitutional values.
- **Structured Assessment:** Systematic evaluation through board examinations and continuous assessments.

5. Importance of National Boards

National Boards play a vital role in ensuring quality education and preparing students to contribute to the nation's development. They maintain standardised academic frameworks, promote equity in education, and foster a sense of national identity and unity. By offering structured education and evaluation systems, national boards ensure that students are academically competent and socially responsible.

6. Challenges Faced by National Boards

- Large disparity in quality among different boards and schools.
- Pressure of examination-oriented education.
- Need for curriculum updates to meet global standards.
- Infrastructure gaps, especially in rural areas.

CBSE (Central Board of Secondary Education)

1. Introduction

The **Central Board of Secondary Education (CBSE)** is one of the most prominent national-level education boards in India. It functions under the control of the **Ministry of Education, Government of India**. Established in **1962**, CBSE is responsible for regulating and supervising school education in India. It affiliates schools across the country and abroad, ensuring a uniform standard of education.

CBSE is known for its **scientifically designed curriculum**, emphasis on **core subjects** like Science, Mathematics, and English, and its role in preparing students for national-level entrance examinations.

2. Objectives of CBSE

The main objectives of CBSE include:

- To prescribe uniform curricula and examination patterns across affiliated schools.
- To promote national integration through education.
- To provide stress-free, child-centred, and holistic education.
- To prepare students for higher education and competitive examinations.
- To integrate innovations in teaching-learning methodologies with psychological and pedagogical principles.

3. Structure and Administration

CBSE is headed by a **Chairperson**, assisted by academic, administrative, and examination committees. It functions through its regional offices located in different parts of India. The board affiliates:

- Kendriya Vidyalayas (KVs)
- Jawahar Navodaya Vidyalayas (JNVs)
- Private schools
- Schools run by central government organisations like the Railways and Defence

4. Functions of CBSE

a) Curriculum Design

CBSE prepares syllabi for Classes 1 to 12. Its curriculum is aligned with **NCERT** textbooks and emphasises competency-based and skill-oriented learning.

b) Conducting Examinations

CBSE conducts major national-level examinations:

- **All India Secondary School Examination (AISSE – Class 10)**
- **All India Senior School Certificate Examination (AISSCE – Class 12)**
- **Joint Entrance Examination (JEE – Main)** for engineering admissions (earlier).
- **NEET-UG** for medical admissions (until NTA took over).

c) Affiliation of Schools

CBSE grants affiliation to schools across India and abroad, ensuring they follow its curriculum and norms.

d) Evaluation and Reforms

The board introduces innovative reforms in evaluation, such as Continuous and Comprehensive Evaluation (CCE), competency-based assessment, and recently **Class 10 & 12 board exam reforms under NEP 2020**.

e) Inclusive Education

CBSE promotes inclusive practices by providing special provisions for differently-abled students, skill-based subjects, and multilingual learning.

5. CBSE and NEP 2020

With the implementation of **National Education Policy (NEP) 2020**, CBSE is:

- Introducing **competency-based questions** in board exams.
- Moving towards a **modular and flexible exam structure**.
- Integrating **artificial intelligence, coding, and vocational education** in curricula.
- Promoting **skill development** along with academic excellence.

6. Importance of CBSE

CBSE plays a central role in Indian education by:

- Offering a **nationally uniform curriculum** recognised across India and abroad.
- Preparing students for competitive exams and higher education.

- Ensuring holistic development by integrating academics with co-curricular activities.
- Acting as a model board in adopting **modern pedagogy and assessment methods**.

State Boards of Education

1. Introduction

State Boards of Education are educational authorities established by the respective state governments in India to regulate, manage, and develop school education within the state. Each state and union territory has its own education board that designs curricula, conducts examinations, and prescribes textbooks for schools affiliated to it. These boards primarily govern education from primary to higher secondary level, focusing on regional requirements, language, and socio-cultural aspects.

State Boards play a vital role in decentralizing the education system of India by catering to the specific needs of local communities while aligning with national education policies.

2. Objectives of State Boards

The key objectives of the State Boards are:

- **Curriculum Development:** To design syllabi that reflect both national guidelines and regional priorities.

- **Examinations:** To conduct secondary (Class 10) and higher secondary (Class 12) public examinations.
- **Textbook Publication:** To prescribe, publish, and distribute textbooks for affiliated schools.
- **Teacher Development:** To conduct training, workshops, and orientation programmes for teachers.
- **Inclusion of Regional Contexts:** To integrate local culture, history, and language into the curriculum.
- **Implementation of Policies:** To ensure execution of state and national education policies such as RTE Act, NEP 2020, etc.

3. Structure of State Boards

Each state board functions under the **Department/Ministry of Education of the respective state government**. The structure generally includes:

- **Chairperson or President** – Head of the board, responsible for policy decisions.
- **Secretary/Controller of Examinations** – Supervises administrative work and examination processes.
- **Academic Committee** – Designs curriculum, teaching methods, and evaluation systems.
- **Examination Committee** – Conducts and regulates board examinations.
- **Finance Committee** – Manages budget, resources, and infrastructural development.

4. Functions of State Boards

a) Curriculum & Syllabus Design

- Formulating curriculum in line with NCERT/SCERT guidelines and state requirements.

b) Examinations & Certification

- Conducting Class 10 (Secondary School) and Class 12 (Higher Secondary) exams.
- Granting certificates recognized nationally and internationally.

c) Textbook Preparation

- Publishing textbooks in state/regional languages to ensure inclusivity.

d) Educational Research & Development

- Encouraging innovative teaching methods and evaluation techniques.

e) Implementation of Schemes

- Executing central and state schemes such as **Mid-Day Meal, RMSA, SSA**, and digital initiatives.

5. Role of State Boards under NEP 2020

The **National Education Policy (NEP) 2020** emphasizes:

- Holistic and multidisciplinary education.
- Reducing rote learning and focusing on conceptual understanding.
- Using the mother tongue/regional language as a medium of instruction at least till Grade 5.
- Promoting vocational and skill-based education. State Boards are expected to redesign syllabi, integrate digital learning, and ensure alignment with national goals while addressing regional diversity.

6. Importance of State Boards

- **Accessibility:** Provide education opportunities to rural and semi-urban students.
- **Affordability:** Generally lower fee structures compared to central boards.
- **Cultural Relevance:** Curriculum reflects regional culture, history, and values.
- **Language Promotion:** Encourage learning in state languages, enhancing inclusivity.
- **Equity:** Ensure education reaches diverse socio-economic groups.

www.ingramcontent.com/pod-product-compliance
Lightning Source LLC
Chambersburg PA
CBHW062103160726
48282CB00026B/656